Twayne's United States Authors Series

Sylvia E. Bowman, *Editor*

INDIANA UNIVERSITY

Paul Hamilton Hayne

PAUL HAMILTON HAYNE

By **RAYBURN S. MOORE**

University of Georgia

(TUSAS) 202

Twayne Publishers, Inc.   ::   New York

For Jay B. Hubbell

and

For my parents

Preface

This study is the first book-length treatment of Paul Hamilton Hayne's poetry. There are, of course, theses and dissertations on various aspects of Hayne's life and work, and Kate H. Becker's *Paul Hamilton Hayne: Life and Letters* (1951) offers a summary "compiled" from already published materials. Far more valuable are the collections of letters and correspondence edited by D. M. McKeithan and Charles Duffy and the discussions of Hayne as critic and man of letters by Jay B. Hubbell and Edd W. Parks. Hayne's poetry, however, has hitherto never been fully considered.

After sketching his life and literary career, I have therefore concentrated on Hayne as poet by considering his collections in turn (including one put together after his death by his wife and son) and by discussing the more important poems in each. Since few of these pieces have been treated in any detail by twentieth-century critics, I have examined all the major collections of Hayne papers (particularly those in the chief repository at Perkins Library, Duke University) and have tried to present certain basic facts regarding the composition, publication, and the then contemporary criticism of both individual poems and collections. Moreover, I have drawn comparisons and traced developments in Hayne's ideas and techniques. I have, wherever possible, let his poems speak for themselves because they are not well known, nor are they available in paperback editions or readily accessible in many libraries. There is not, however, sufficient space to subject individual poems to full-scale critical analysis, but within the contextual limits of this approach, I have been critical withal.*

I have sought neither to make a case for Hayne as a major poet

---

* Since this was written (May, 1967), more stringent stipulations regarding space have forced me to cut documentation and bibliography rigorously and to prune quoted materials considerably.

of the nineteenth century nor to ignore his faults and weaknesses. Despite the high esteem in which his poetry was held by some in his own day, it has not stood well the test of time; and Hayne is presently regarded as being more important to literary history as a man of letters than as a poet. However, Maurice Thompson's assertion of 1883 should not be overlooked today: "Whoever would read the literary history of America, in the works of her truest literary artificers, can not afford to pass the poems of Paul H. Hayne by." There remains a germ of truth in this statement, though Hayne no longer seems one of the "truest literary artificers." As the "Poet Laureate of the South," as a nineteenth-century American poet in the mainstream of English poetic tradition, as a sincere and devoted servant of the muse working under conditions far from ideal, and as the author of a substantial body of melodious and competently contrived verse, Hayne deserves the attention of modern scholarship. I have therefore sought to give him his due by providing a general critical consideration of his poetry. Such a study is not likely to win Hayne new fame or laurels, but it does at least give his verse in both range and particulars a long overdue hearing. The rest depends upon the poems themselves.

Athens, Georgia

RAYBURN S. MOORE

Acknowledgments

It is a pleasure to record here the obligations I have incurred in writing this book. Without the gracious cooperation of the staff of Perkins Library, Duke University, this study would have been impossible, and I should like therefore to express my deep appreciation to Benjamin E. Powell, J. P. Waggoner, Florence Blakely, Mary Canada, Elvin Strowd, Emerson Ford, Virginia Gray, Dan McGrath, and, above all, to Mattie Russell, Curator of Manuscripts, who made it possible for me to examine the indispensable Hayne Collection under ideal working conditions.

Other libraries have also been helpful. Porter Kellam and the staff of the University of Georgia Library—especially Christine Burroughs, Gloria McDaniel, Anne Thompson, John Bonner, Marvin Sexton, and Paul Spence—have been unfailingly kind and helpful. E. L. Inabinett and his assistants in manuscripts at the South Caroliniana Library of the University of South Carolina were hospitable. I am also grateful to the libraries of Ohio State University, University of Tennessee, University of Alabama, University of Missouri, Emory University, Duke University, Tulane University, Princeton University, Dartmouth College, Oberlin College, and Harvard University (Baker Library) for making materials available to me through interlibrary loan and to the Alderman Library of the University of Virginia, the Houghton Library of Harvard University, the Milton S. Eisenhower Library of the Johns Hopkins University, the Ella Strong Denison Library of Scripps College, the Friends Historical Library of Swarthmore College, the Library of Congress, the New York Public Library, the Perkins Library of Duke University, and the historical societies of Massachusetts, Wisconsin, and Pennsylvania for reproducing letters and manuscripts and permitting me to quote from them.

I should like to offer my thanks for various scholarly courtesies to Frank Durham, James Black, Gayle Ingram, Barbara Sullivan, John Riley, Marie Bradley, Harriet Holman, Griffith Pugh, Margaret Moore, and D. M. McKeithan. I am particularly grateful to Jay B. Hubbell, John O. Eidson, and Edd W. Parks for reading drafts of the book and contributing valuable suggestions and criticism. Edd Parks, alas, is no longer here to receive my salute, but I should like to acknowledge a general and generous debt to him as scholar and colleague.

I am indebted to Robert H. West, John O. Eidson, and Robert A. McRorie for making it possible for me to devote parts of each year from 1964 to 1967 to this work. I wish also to thank Clarence Gohdes, Arlin Turner, and Charles Predmore for a summer grant in 1964 from the Graduate School of Duke University.

My chief debt is to Jay B. Hubbell, who, years ago as my teacher and advisor, first called my attention to Hayne and to the important collection of papers bearing his name at Duke University. I have tried to express my gratitude and to suggest my admiration and affection through the dedication of this study.

For permission to quote from their publications, I should like to thank the following editors and publishers: To W. W. Davidson and the *Georgia Review* for allowing me to reprint much of my article on Hayne; to Ralph Stephens and the University of Georgia Press for passages in *Georgians in Profile* (1958); to the Johns Hopkins Press for passages from *The Centennial Edition of the Works of Sidney Lanier* (1945); to the University of Texas Press for passages from *A Collection of Hayne Letters* (1944); to Vanderbilt University Press for passages from *Essays in Honor of Walter Clyde Curry* (1955); and to Ashbel G. Brice and Duke University Press for passages from Jay B. Hubbell's *The Last Years of Henry Timrod* (1941) and *The South in American Literature* (1954).

Contents

Chronology

1830   Paul Hamilton Hayne born in Charleston, South Carolina, January 1.

1840's Attends Classical School of Christopher Cotes.

1845   First verse published in *Charleston Courier.*

1847   Attends College of Charleston and graduates in 1850.

1852   Studies law; in May, marries Mary Middleton Michel.

1854   *Poems* (1855) published in Boston.

1857   *Sonnets, and Other Poems.* Edits *Russell's Magazine* until 1860.

1859   *Avolio* (1860), collected edition of early poems.

1861   On staff of Governor Francis Pickens until March, 1862.

1862– Contributes to Confederate periodicals.

1865

1866   Moves to Augusta, Georgia. Health breaks. Settles family at Copse Hill and contributes anew to Northern magazines.

1872   *Legends and Lyrics,* first postwar collection.

1873   Edits *Poems of Henry Timrod.*

1875   *The Mountain of the Lovers.*

1882   *Poems.* Complete Edition. Last collection.

1886   Health fails; dies July 6 and is buried July 11 in public ceremony in Augusta.

CHAPTER 1

A Biographical Sketch[1]

I *Birth and Boyhood*

PAUL Hamilton Hayne was born January 1, 1830, in Charleston, South Carolina, the only child of Lt. Paul Hamilton Hayne (1803–31), an officer in the United States Navy and member of a prominent Carolina family devoted to public service, and Emily McElhenny Hayne (1806–79), the daughter of a Presbyterian minister. After his father's promising naval career was cut short by yellow fever, the boy was reared by his mother with the help of one of his uncles, Robert Y. Hayne, Daniel Webster's redoubtable opponent in the famous Senate debate on nullification in 1830. This was an important factor in his upbringing, since Emily Hayne was grief-stricken by her husband's early death and withdrew austerely into herself and the past. His uncle, though busy with politics and business, became a formative influence in his life and served as his guardian: he taught him to ride, hunt, and shoot; laid down certain principles of polity and honor; and provided two sons as companions. But Robert Y. Hayne died in 1839, and the lad thereby lost a second father, the depth of his admiration and affection finding expression years later in a long biographical sketch (1878) and in "My Mother-Land" (1862), a poem celebrating Carolina, its history and its cause, in which the elder Hayne is viewed as a champion of "Right" in the "lists of eloquence" against Webster, the "proud Bois Guilbert of debate."

II *Education*

As a child, Hayne attended the Classical School of Christopher Cotes (frequently spelled Coates or Coats), where he sat next to Henry Timrod, exchanged ballads with him, and soon became his fast friend. There Hayne studied history, mathematics, and the classics; engaged in "shinny" and other schoolboy sports; and read Simms's romances and Timrod's first poems on the sly. For this extracurricular activity he was caned by one of his teachers. But his interest in literature did not diminish. He read the *Arabian Nights,* the *Swiss Family Robinson,* Scott's and Dickens' novels, the old English ballads, and Froissart's *Chronicles.* His favorite book was *Robinson Crusoe,* a story he read over and over again, often aloud to his mother, until he believed in the "veritable existence of 'Robin' and his 'man Friday'" and "wore out" the book by "*eternal* handling." [2]

Yet he was not a complete introvert. He "passionately and persistently" hunted ducks, quail, and deer, and he took "keen delight" in following the hounds. Horseback riding was one of his greatest pleasures, and he considered himself a "born Nomad" whose nature demanded that he "scour" the woodlands and "gallop" along the "solitary by-roads." The nearby ocean provided another world of sport for him—boating, swimming, fishing, and walking on the beaches. He also liked to travel and looked forward each year to visits to his mother's upcountry plantation and to places even farther away.

In the summer of 1843 he took his first long trip. With his mother and one of his aunts he went by boat to New York and traveled to Northampton and New Haven by train and coach. He enjoyed the ocean voyage, thought New York Harbor beautiful, and admired Broadway. Late in July the little group went to Northampton. There the lad took French from a private tutor and was taught other subjects by his mother. He sketched the Connecticut River at Mount Holyoke and watched silkworms in a "coocoonery." In September he practiced his French by conversing with a Frenchman who boarded at the same house in New Haven; had fun rowing with friends on the river two miles away; and was impressed by the handsome churches and local customs.

Returning to Charleston later in the fall, he resumed his studies and wrote poems for the edification of his mother and Cousin Sue. Mrs. Hayne encouraged him, and his first published poem—"The Ashley at the Battery"—appeared appropriately enough in a Charleston newspaper in 1845. In the same year Timrod left town to enter the University of Georgia at a time when he and Hayne might have found each other's criticism beneficial.

Less than two years later Hayne himself escaped Cotes's malacca cane by matriculating at the College of Charleston. He could not, however, avoid his first serious malady, a "severe fever of a nervo-billious kind"; but, despite ill health, he won prizes in English composition and elocution and delivered an oration at the graduation exercises of his class on February 26, 1850.

After leaving college, Hayne took an interest in politics as an active supporter of Robert Barnwell Rhett and secession; and, for a few months in the fall of 1851, he contributed to the *Palmetto Flag,* a short-lived paper established to promote secession. At his mother's urging, he also took up the study of the law in the office of James Louis Petigru, opposer of nullification and uncompromising Unionist, who was one of the leading legal minds of the state. Although Hayne was later admitted to the bar, he was more interested in literature. He had begun contributing to the *Southern Literary Messenger* in 1848 and had become associate editor of the *Southern Literary Gazette* in May, 1852. By the following December, he had taken over the management of the *Gazette* for a debt of $800 owed him and had given up the law to devote his energies to his journal.

III *Young Poet and Editor*

Though Hayne changed the title to the *Weekly News and Literary Gazette,* treated his contributors courteously (one later praised him for accepting articles as they were written and for not assuming "'editorial airs'"), and appealed to his readers for better financial support, the publication continued to lose money and died within a year. In the meantime, he turned to collecting his poems and journeyed north to Boston in 1853 to seek a publisher. Encouraged by his reception, he engaged Ticknor and Fields to publish his verse and returned in the late summer of 1854 to see a small edition through the press. There he discoursed on friendly terms with Longfellow, Lowell, Emerson, Whipple, Holmes, and other literary men. He enjoyed these acquaintances (especially E. P. Whipple whom he regarded as "a sort of father"), but in his daily routine he felt that he was not "at home" and, indeed, that he was "an alien & sojourner in the land."

James T. Fields, a partner in the publishing firm and a literary man himself, praised Hayne's poems as being "full of the richest fancy," but he still charged $180 for an edition of five hundred copies, a sum Hayne had to get up with the financial assistance of his mother. Despite this problem and the long hours he spent correcting proof in Fields's "dingy little office," Hayne decided to make literature his career, "not exclusively so, perhaps," he admitted in October, 1854, "(for I must make it subsidiary to some lucrative employment) but still in a great measure my heart & soul shall be in that work." Within a year he was writing for a number of periodicals, including *Graham's Magazine* and the *Home Journal*; and the "divine itch" had become "constitutional."

Meanwhile, on the day before he became associate editor of the *Southern Literary Gazette* in 1852, he married, after an engagement of less than a year, Mary Middleton Michel, daughter of a prominent French physician in Charleston. If he had not seriously considered a literary career before his marriage, he certainly did afterward; for "Minna" Hayne thought highly of him as a poet and devoted herself to encouraging and promoting his ambitions. The dedicatory sonnet to his first volume of verse acknowledges his debt to her, the "dear Angel" and "gentle Critic" of his "cherished home," an acknowledgment he repeated often throughout his life.

Poems (1855), when it appeared in November, 1854, was generally well received by those critics who noticed it at all. Whipple, for example, described it as containing "nothing puny in thought, nothing puerile in the feeling, nothing conceited in the expression"; altogether, he felt it to be a collection of "great promise as well as fine performance."

Encouraged by this review and a few others, including one by Richard Henry Stoddard—a young New York poet, critic, and a recent acquaintance—if not by the book's commercial success (over a hundred copies were sold in Charleston, but the sale elsewhere was negligible), Hayne set to work in earnest; and, despite periods of ill health, his own or his wife's, trips to Georgia, New York, and Florida, and the birth of a son in March, he had enough poems for another volume by the fall of 1856. Since the publication of *Poems* in Boston had occasioned some unfavorable criticism in Charleston, *Sonnets, and Other Poems* was published early in 1857 by Harper & Calvo, a local firm. Three hundred copies were issued, but less than two hundred were sold, for Hayne still had "more than 100" on his own library shelves two and a half years later.

In the summer of 1856 Hayne agreed to become editor of *Russell's Magazine,* an organ of "Southern intellect, taste, and opinions" and a monthly soon to be launched "much upon the plan of Blackwood." John Russell, a Charleston bookseller, undertook to pay the expenses, and the local literati, Simms and Timrod among them, consented to contribute. In order to get "Maga," as he usually called it, off to a good start, Hayne spent some weeks in the fall and winter of 1856–57 lecturing in the upcountry of South Carolina and the lower part of North Carolina. *Russell's* managed to last three years, largely because of Hayne's Herculean efforts to keep it going and the willingness of many contributors to write for nothing (Hayne himself assuredly never received anything for his services). [3]

During parts of this period, to be sure, Hayne was not in Charleston. In search of better health for all, he and his family spent the summers of 1858 in Virginia and of 1860 in Aiken, South Carolina. Hayne himself took Minna Hayne to Philadelphia in 1859 to consult a physician. On March 29, 1859, he wrote Stoddard: "Without referring to my *own health* which has been (at times) very feeble, I have only to tell you that my wife . . . has been repeatedly at death's door. . . . Thank God! we are *both* better *now.* . . . My disease has been a cross between the *liver*-complaint common in these low latitudes, and the *lung*-complaint, which is common at the North" (*Letters,* 33).

Despite ill health and the endless editorial problems and the often precarious financial condition of *Russell's,* Hayne prepared a new edition of his verse and subsidized its publication by Ticknor and Fields. *Avolio: A Legend of the Island of Cos. With Poems, Lyrical, Miscellaneous, and Dramatic* (1860) appeared in November, 1859, and was kindly received by Lowell in the *Atlantic* and by Bryant in the *Evening Post.* Whipple remarked on the poet's "intellectual growth" in his review in the Boston *Evening Transcript.* The time seemed ripe for Hayne to take his rightful place in the group of young bards—Stoddard, E. C. Stedman, T. B. Aldrich, W. D. Howells, among them—who were beginning to be heard in the land, but the political situation of 1860 contributed to the demise of *Russell's,* and Hayne embraced his state's cause with alacrity.

IV　The Civil War

As a hot secessionist from his youth and as the nephew of the spokesman of Nullification, Hayne supported South Carolina's withdrawal from the Union and was present for the engrossing of the Ordinance of Secession in Charleston on December 20, 1860. Early in 1861 Hayne became an aide to Governor Francis Pickens, a stepbrother of his mother's, since his health was too delicate for service in the field. In this capacity he served at Fort Sumter from November to March, 1862; but even these duties proved too arduous for him. Consequently, he retired to his study and later to various upcountry villages to support the Confederacy with his pen. His poems appeared in newspapers and magazines throughout the South, but he never matched the achievement of Timrod as a war poet. During this period he also lectured on occasion in behalf of one Confederate organization or another, and he found time to review the English poets from Chaucer to Tennyson and to read the prose of Sir Thomas Browne and Leigh Hunt and the fiction of Scott, Dickens, Dumas, Reade, Charlotte Brontë, and George Eliot. He did not, however, confine himself exclusively to composing war poems. One of his chief efforts of 1864 was the "Wife of Brittany," a long narrative based on Chaucer's "Franklin's Tale," which was not published until 1870.

Though Hayne did not have to face the hazard of shot and shell, he had to confront another bitter experience—the defeat of the Confederacy and its consequences. The war ruined him in "fortune & prospects." His home and much of his library were burned; his mother's property was heavily damaged; silver and other valuables were stolen; and the family investments in Confederate bonds and securities were lost. Not only was a cause lost but also a way of life and the wherewithal to support it.

V　Aftermath

Sick at heart and spirit and poverty-stricken, Hayne went to Augusta, Georgia, in July, 1865, and became news editor of the *Constitutionalist* at $20 a week. He worked ten hours a day and found the detail "troublesome," though he took pleasure in being able to support himself. "No human being," he wrote his wife on August 6, 1865, "could imagine what I suffered of torture & humiliation at the Gov'n's [Francis Pickens'] house & having known what it is, to eat the bitter bread of dependence, my exultation at escaping from such bondage is only the more intense."

Despite his limited means (he resigned from the newspaper in October and worked on it only intermittently thereafter), he collected his wife, son, and a few belongings and moved in April, 1866, into Hayne's Roost, a "small white-washed cottage rudely built of unseasoned lumber and clap-boards of pine" surrounded by eighteen acres of pine and fruit trees on top of a hill sixteen miles from Augusta on the Georgia Railroad. Emily Hayne joined them before the year ended, and Edmund Bailey, a young Negro hired to do odd jobs, soon made a place for himself in the household as cook and friend to Will.

At "Copse Hill," as he later called it, Hayne resolved anew, with the encouragement of his wife, to devote himself to literary pursuits, a resolution he kept until his death in spite of illness, poverty, and disappointment. Occasionally, as in a letter of 1866 to an unnamed correspondent, he was inclined to rail eloquently at the hard lot he had to bear: "here at the South a man of literary tastes is looked down upon by the generality of people—aye! even by gentlemen of some culture and unquestionable social position as a mere *idle* Dreamer, an unpractical fool, a drone in the great business hive, a species of Pariah, against whom every dry goods' Clerk & cloth-yard Apprentice is privileged to launch the small arrows of his scorn & ridicule!"

VI   *The Struggle for Bread*

Despite Hayne's disheartening circumstances, he at once sought to reestablish communication with his literary friends in the North. In 1866 he wrote Fields, Holmes, and Stoddard in the hope that they might be able to sell his poems to Northern magazines. With occasional help and often without—Fields, now editor of the *Atlantic,* rejected his offerings—he sold verse in the 1860's to *Appletons' Journal, Lippincott's Magazine,* the *Galaxy,* the *Old Guard,* the *Round Table,* and others. At the same time, he was contributing to many Southern periodicals, few of which were long-lived or able to pay for contributions. Nevertheless, he managed to establish himself on a precarious financial basis and by the end of the year was able to provide his family with a "cuisine" of potatoes, partridges, bacon, and eggs, as well as with claret for the table and "good old Rye" for himself.

His routine was simple: composition and reading during the day, varied by long walks, woodcutting, hunting (he especially enjoyed shooting quail), and at night long sessions of letter writing, keeping a journal or diary up to date, or reading aloud to the family. Willie and Edmund recited their lessons to him, though Willie as often as not was allowed to "go wild" among his father's "literary 'preserves' " and to read after his own inclination according to "Dr. Johnson's plan." Edmund he taught to read Virgil.

"One can go clothed in an old dressing gown," Hayne noted in his diary in 1866, without "fear of duns, or visitors. Peace reigns supreme." Yet he was genuinely liked by his neighbors and was usually addressed as Colonel in keeping with the old Southern custom regarding titles and in acknowledgment of his former rank as Governor Pickens' aide. Though Hayne was pleased that there was no need for show or "humbug of any kind"—for his "scanty exchequer" could ill afford the usual "social drains"—he grew restive at his isolation and wrote to Simms, Timrod, Stoddard, and Bayard Taylor to come for a visit. He could not, he acknowledged, entertain on the scale of the old days in Charleston; but he offered the "*warmest, if homeliest of welcomes*" and a share of what he had in the way of ideas, tobacco, "mountain-dew," and "bird-music." Simms and Timrod accepted his invitations.

When Simms paid his visit during the Christmas season of 1866, he found his friend's surroundings "rather a melancholy sight," but the reunion was a pleasant one despite a fare of bacon and hardtack and the absence of Madeira. Timrod, who came the following May and returned in August, liked the climate—the "light, bracing, aromatic pine-land atmosphere"—enjoyed the "communion" with the "dearest" of his friends and considered Copse Hill a second home. Shortly after his second visit, Timrod died; Simms lived less than three years thereafter; and Hayne was thus bereft of his oldest and closest literary friends in Charleston. [4]

The first years in Georgia were often difficult for other reasons than those connected with poverty and the deaths of comrades. Minna Hayne's frail constitution could not readily adjust to the rigors of living under such crude conditions, and Hayne too was frequently ill—indeed, he had recurrent hemorrhages and bouts with "biliousness" and shortness of breath for the rest of his life. His journals and letters give abundant testimony to these trials, and it is no wonder that many of his comments bewail his fate. "It only happens," he explained to a friend, "when some particular piece of outside ill luck coincides with an attack of illness; when Literature & The Liver (to indulge in personification) begin to 'pitch into me,' one from the right, tother from the left—that flesh and blood giving way for the moment, I indulge in a stentorian 'cuss' . . . , a dismal howl, or a series of lamentable whimpers. . . ." Yet he was not unaware that others might be even more unfortunate, as he indicates in a journal entry for March 20, 1866: "But a truce to whining. I'm a little too fond of pitying myself. Let me think of my poor wife, so constant, faithful, heroic!"

In June, 1867, Hayne became literary editor of *Southern Opinion,* a post he held for two years on the Richmond journal; and in the following December he became a regular contributor to *Southern Society,* a short-lived Baltimore weekly which took two columns of prose an issue and an occasional poem for $8.00 per week. But these periodicals were both on an uncertain financial footing; and, when the *Opinion* folded in 1869, he could not collect "about 500 dollars" due him, so he decided to free-lance. As he wrote Simms on April 29, "Only by becoming an absolute free lance, or a Bohemian of Letters, can a man of my *light calibre* make his bread now-a-days. Fame, posthumous renown . . . I must leave to my intellectual betters . . ." (*Letters,* 213–14).

In the meantime, life improved at Copse Hill, and Hayne became more reconciled to his lot. "Indeed," he admitted to Simms on May 17, 1869: "I have come to consider my position fortunate. *Leisure* I can command in abundance—many of the new books, and all the best periodicals, (English & American) reach me. I have nothing whatever to do with the wretched turmoil of cities, and as for politics, & tyranny, . . . except as they reach me faintly thro the papers—, [they] are disregarded & unheard! Yes, had I but *health,* I should be that *rara avis*—a contented mortal!" Good health, however, was something he could not "command," he explained to Simms in the following December. In response to Simms's description of his physical complaints, Hayne expounded on his own "dyspepsia" and "nerves" (*Letters,* 224).

Nevertheless, despite his health and his inadequate income, Hayne made plans in the fall of 1870, so he wrote Whipple in October, to visit Boston the following spring. The trip was delayed, however, for Hayne's financial situation was still precarious, his health was erratic, and he was anxious to publish the poems of the last decade (his most mature output to date) before returning in person to the Northern literary centers. Accordingly, he turned his efforts toward securing a publisher for his uncollected verse.

VII   *First Postwar Books*

As early as 1866 Hayne had begun collecting his poems for a new volume, but he had difficulty finding a publisher who was willing to risk such a venture without financial support from the author, and Hayne was too poor to pay the normal costs of publication. Finally, after trying a number of firms in New York and Boston, he worked out a compromise with J. B. Lippincott of Philadelphia in the fall of 1871. When *Legends and Lyrics* appeared in January, 1872, it was favorably reviewed in Boston, New York, and Philadelphia, as well as in the South. In the *Evening Transcript* for February 5, 1872, Whipple characterized Hayne as the "most eminent of living Southern poets" and cited the book as containing the "ripest results" of the writer's genius.

Hayne, however, was not content merely to publish his own work. He was eager also for Timrod to have a hearing, belated though it might be. Indeed, from the time of Timrod's death in 1867, Hayne had been interested in editing his friend's poems and in writing a biography of him. After approaching a number of publishers on such a volume, he finally in April, 1872, "induced" the New York firm of E. J. Hale and Son to undertake it. By September the manuscript was ready, and in the following January the book appeared.

A "labor of love" to the editor, the *Poems of Henry Timrod* seeks as a whole to present Timrod's life and work in the best light from the point of view of an advocate and close friend. The disadvantages of such an approach are obvious: but, as Edd W. Parks observed in *Henry Timrod* (1964), the editing of the poems is "scrupulous, if not quite impeccable," and the memoir is "in reality a warm-hearted yet discerning tribute to a friend and fellow poet" (108–9).

The response to the volume was immediate and favorable. A second, enlarged edition was ready in April. Longfellow and Whittier expressed their praise in letters, and many commendatory notices appeared in the Northern press, Hayne's favorite being a long review by Stoddard in the *Aldine* for April, 1873. Mrs. Timrod was pleased, and Hayne felt that he had served his friend's memory well. He had brought "Hal's" life and poetry to the attention of the public throughout the country and had "moved" readers to consider Timrod's verse, he wrote Margaret J. Preston on April 13, 1873, "with an indulgence, and almost a loving gentleness, which could not otherwise have been elicited." This consideration, after all, was what he had really wished to achieve. Now he was free to make the trip to Boston and to other Northern cities that he had postponed in 1870.

VIII   *Journey to the North*

Desiring to check personally his royalty account at Lippincott and to meet or renew acquaintance with editors and correspondents, Hayne traveled north in the summer of 1873 for the first time since the late 1850's; and, though he received little satisfaction from his publisher, the trip was a success in terms of prestige and pleasure. He took Will with him, and they stopped off for brief stays with friends in North Carolina, Washington, D.C., Baltimore, and Philadelphia; conferred with editors and publishers in New York and Boston; visited Longfellow on several occasions, saw R. H. Dana, and spent several days with Whittier; received calls from Holmes and also from Howells and Fields, both of whom invited father and son to be their guests; and enjoyed the warm reception (a "kind of ovation," as he characterized it in letters home) accorded them wherever they went. But, in New York near the end of his sojourn, Hayne injured his ankle in stepping from a streetcar, was confined to bed for six weeks, and underwent two "surgical operations." Even in such adversity the hospitality continued. Whittier, Longfellow, and Bryant lent financial assistance; publishers James R. Osgood and Joseph W. Harper proffered loans; and the *Independent* and the *Chris-*

tian Union both advanced large sums against future Hayne contributions. He was touched by these exhibitions of concern and never forgot these generous actions.

He was somewhat "lame" after his return to Copse Hill, though he acknowledged to Mrs. Preston on December 23, 1873, that the "paroxysms of agony in the foot & leg have disappeared." "Now," he added, "the only trouble is, that I cannot straighten fully the injured limb."

Nevertheless, he set about seeking a publisher for another collection of his poems. By the spring of 1874 several firms had declined to accept the manuscript because Hayne did not wish to undertake any of the expense of publication. Finally, *The Mountain of the Lovers; with Poems of Nature and Tradition* was brought out in June, 1875, by E. J. Hale and Son, the publisher of his edition of Timrod's poems.

Life at Copse Hill continued the even tenor of its ways. Surrounded by books and magazines, Hayne worked regularly at his standing desk, interrupted only by intermittent illness or depression. He enjoyed the usual pleasures of rural life, including his pets, Spot and Brownie, a dog and squirrel, and later Maggie, a horse he named for Mrs. Preston and trained himself. His family remained intact, Will living at home and visiting relatives in Charleston and Montgomery regularly and Emily Hayne staying until her death in December, 1879.

During the 1870's Hayne carried on a voluminous correspondence with many American and British writers—Longfellow, Whittier, Holmes, Bryant, Whipple, Stedman, Howells, Taylor, Lanier, Cooke, Thompson, Mrs. Preston, and Constance Fenimore Woolson, among the Americans; and with Swinburne, Charles Reade, R. D. Blackmore, Jean Ingelow, William Black, and Philip Bourke Marston, among the British. Hayne's poems and prose appeared from time to time in *Harper's Monthly, Lippincott's, Scribner's Monthly, Appletons' Journal, Youth's Companion,* the *Atlantic,* the *Galaxy,* and other influential Northern magazines. He also contributed to numerous Southern periodicals—the *Southern Magazine,* the *Sunny South,* and the *South Atlantic,* to mention only a few. [5]

IX   *Second Trip North*

After another long illness, Hayne sought a change in climate, and with his wife made his last journey north in the summer of 1879. They went to Washington, Philadelphia, New York, Boston, and various resorts in New England. They vacationed in the White Mountains where Hayne fished and rested. They spent five days as Whittier's guests and became intimates of the household; had lunch with Longfellow; received a call from Holmes and attended his "first lecture" of the term; "passed an evening" with Whipple; and visited a week each with new and wealthy friends, the Charles A. Coffins in Lynn, Massachusetts, and the Rowland G. Hazards in Newport, Rhode Island.

Despite Hayne's pleasure in such good company, he had "several hemorrhages" during the summer, the most severe of which occurred in New York City in October. There he was cheered by the attentions of his old friends Stedman and Stoddard and of new ones like Edgar Fawcett and Francis S. Saltus, young esthetes, bohemians, and acquaintances by correspondence. Hayne returned home late in the month feeling stronger and buoyed up by the hope that the collected edition of his poems—proposed in 1878 and promoted by his friend John Garland James, a Virginia-born Texas educator—would be heavily subscribed. Though the edition failed as a subscription project, the Boston firm of D. Lothrop and Company agreed in November, 1880, to assume the risks of publication, at least partially because of the number (more than two hundred) and prestige of the subscribers—Longfellow, Whittier, Holmes, Whipple, Stedman, G. H. Boker, and many lesser literary figures, to say nothing of prominent military leaders, politicians, ministers, and scholars—James had previously obtained.

X *Honors*

Lothrop brought out the *Poems* in the fall of 1882. The critics found good things to say about the collection, though there was some disagreement about the author's stature as a poet. One, for example, characterized him as a "foremost living American poet," but another considered him entitled rather to an "honourable place among the minor poets."

Regardless of his rank, Hayne was by this time known throughout the country and was appealed to for autographs and poems. He was asked to write odes and lyrics for various public occasions: the centennials of the battle of King's Mountain in 1880, of the British surrender at Yorktown in 1881, of the incorporation of Charleston as a city in 1883, of Washington Irving's birth in 1883, and the sesquicentennial of the founding of the colony of Georgia in 1883. He was also asked to provide suitable poems for ceremonies at Smith College and at the International Cotton Exposition in Atlanta; for birthday tributes to Whittier, Holmes, Longfellow, and Emerson; and for a variety of functions honoring the memory of the Confederacy and its supporters. He was approached about delivering an address at Emory College and a series of lectures at Vanderbilt University and about serving as a member of the Board of Examiners at the University of Georgia. He was elected to honorary membership in literary societies at Princeton, Sewanee, Davidson, and the Citadel and in the historical societies of Alabama and Georgia; and he was awarded an honorary degree by Washington and Lee University in 1882.

XI   *Last Years*

Although Hayne was not happy about the postwar South or about the country at large and although he complained about his lot as a Southern writer, he was not just a bitter old fogey sitting on his front stoop hurling philippics at a later generation which held sacred few things that he loved or treasured. He was disheartened by what he interpreted as signs of a grasping materialism in his region, and he was disgusted by those who appeared willing to forget or ignore the past and to accommodate their views to an explanation of it which condemned everything the Old South had stood for. Southerners like George W. Cable, for example, were in his opinion "renegades" and "traitors" to the South; and Henry W. Grady, a fellow Georgian, was only slightly less suspect for embracing certain Yankee economic and political views in promoting the so-called New South.

Notwithstanding these convictions, Hayne was a pioneer in promoting cultural reconciliation between the sections, and he worked for many years to bring about better relations among literary people. He was not opposed to new ideas and developments in agriculture, industry, or literature so long as they assumed a proper relationship to the living tradition of the field involved. He was indeed a cavalier and perhaps, as Maurice

Thompson has observed, the "last" one, but he never considered everything lost, nor did he ever really give up hope that the best qualities of the old regime—its customs and manners, its standards of loyalty and honor, and its sense of noblesse oblige—would not prevail even in a crass new day.

Nor was he a prophet without honor at home, for both South Carolina and Georgia claimed him; and Charleston, Montgomery, Augusta, Atlanta, Savannah, and Macon paid homage to him. He was known throughout the nation as the laureate of the South, and many prominent Northern writers considered him an important American poet and man of letters. He was also stimulated during this period by correspondence with old friends such as Mrs. Preston and with new ones such as Charles Gayarré, Andrew Adgate Lipscomb, and Wilkie Collins. Gayarré, the elderly Louisiana historian, offered Hayne a receptive and sympathetic ear for his political and cultural views; Lipscomb, former chancellor of the University of Georgia and a prominent Methodist divine, gave him an opportunity to discuss the philosophical and theological ideas which commanded his interest; and Collins, the well-known author of *The Moonstone* and *The Woman in White*, served willingly as the British pole in an Anglo-American line of communication on a variety of literary topics. [6]

Despite these pleasant aspects of his life, Hayne's frail health gradually deteriorated. In addition to his old lung condition, he suffered from an "oppression on the chest," a "strange difficulty of breathing," which, in a letter of May 3, 1881, to Mrs. Preston, he attributed to "nervous exhaustion coupled with dyspepsia." There were, however, periods when he felt better; but these were more frequently interrupted by hemorrhages and by a general "nervous decline" after the fall of 1884. "Troubles of the digestion, of the lungs, of the nerves," he wrote Gayarré on September 25, 1885, "it has been God's will that I should endure"; moreover, he remarked to Lipscomb on October 8, "my old complaint, a species of nervous asthma, which keeps me gasping off & on for hours like a fish out of water . . . is indescribably trying."

The "Arctic diablerie" of the winter of 1885–86 almost finished him "altogether," and he acknowledged on February 4 that his constitution seemed to be "failing." "At 56," he pointed out to Gayarré on March 23, "I am really older than you at 81! & shall probably pass over to the 'majority' long before you do." After

"blacking out" at his desk one Sunday night, he wrote on April 5 t(
R. W. Knott, editor of the *Southern Bivouac,* that he did not be
lieve that his life was "worth 3 months' purchase! perhaps not &
weeks!" Later that month he observed in a letter to his cousir
Susan Hayne that his "whole nervous system had collapsed." Ir
May, he was "assailed by a most debilitating sort of dysentery'
from which he partially recovered in June; but later in the
month he had another "attack of unconsciousness," described by
his physicians as a stroke of paralysis; and he died two weeks
afterward on July 6, 1886. Five days later at the "largest funera'
ever held" in Augusta, Bishop John W. Beckwith of the Episcopal
Church delivered the eulogy; and Hayne's body was laid to rest
in Magnolia Cemetery in a plot given by the city in recognitior
of his service and later marked by a monument honoring his
achievement. [7]

XII   *"The Knightliest of Men"*

In appearance Paul Hamilton Hayne possessed "in a striking
degree," according to a Boston newspaper editor, "the typical
characteristics of the poet" ("the more noticeable," he continued,
"because in strong contrast to the appearance presented by the
later generation of New England literary men who look like
society or business men"). [8] He was slight in build—standing
about five feet, seven inches, and weighing usually around one
hundred and twenty pounds—with dark brown eyes, brown hair,
and an olive complexion. Graceful in movement, mercurial in
temperament, courtly and dignified in manner, he was chivalric
by nature and conviction; a fluent conversationalist, his musical,
well-modulated voice suggested all the qualities of the natural
orator save the power of projection; and he apparently had little
difficulty in charming the ladies. Fond of reminiscence and a
good storyteller with an ample supply of literary and historical
anecdote and a ready sense of humor, he was accepted by men,
gentlemen and Crackers alike.

Though slight in figure and weak in constitution as a result
of chronic illness from an early age and though he had been
reared in a home dominated by women, Hayne was neither ef-
feminate nor easily cowed by physical size or strength. He loved

horses and handled them skillfully (he once remarked that he hoped to find in heaven steeds "after the style of Pegasus"); he enjoyed hunting and fishing until the very last years of his life; and he was an excellent shot with either shotgun or pistol, one of his favorite recreations being target shooting with a pistol.

A gentleman of the Old South, Hayne believed fervently in its ideals of duty, integrity, loyalty, courtesy, and noblesse oblige; and he practiced them sincerely. Honor was important to him, and his conception of it was such that he became involved in several duels both as principal and as second. [9] A "thoroughbred in every fibre," he was, as his friend I. W. Avery, editor of the Atlanta *Evening Capitol,* described him on July 8, 1886, "the knightliest of men" and the exemplar of the "genuine gentleman."

A secessionist in his salad days, Hayne believed in the Lost Cause; and, though he worked long and tirelessly for literary and cultural reconciliation after the war ("literature," he wrote Whittier in 1870, "has no sections"), he was "unreconstructed" in politics at the time of his death. "Self government by the masses" he regarded as the "grossest of humbugs"; no man, however, was quicker to appreciate and acknowledge individual merit in any one, and he denounced oppression wherever he saw it, as is exemplified by his "On the Persecution of the Jews in Russia" (1882) in which he attacked the Czar and pleaded for England and America to unite in condemning that monarch's "atrocities." Hayne saw all the faults of the Gilded Age, and he had few illusions about the achievements or the prospects of a democratic society in America.

In matters of religion, Hayne was for much of his life a rather nominal believer. He took Christian morals and ethics seriously; but, despite his mother's strong reform faith, his wife's daily example, and his own knowledge and love of the Bible, he found certain aspects of Christian theology difficult to accept, especially the doctrines of the sovereignty of God and of "eternal damnation." Nevertheless, he embraced late in life the faith of his family and became a communicant of the Episcopal Church in 1883. He took his vows soberly; and, when he knew he was dying, he was anxious to share his faith. His friends were deeply impressed by his spirituality, as Avery also points out in the previously cited editorial: "But the glory of his character was his innate spiritual feeling. ... Mr. Hayne was profoundly spiritual. To few was this intense phase of his nature disclosed, but it secretly and imperiously dominated his great genius."

A complex human being, then, Hayne certainly was—a noble spirit, as some scholars have remarked—and it may justly be said of him, as he once wrote of Simms, that "the *man* was greater than his *works*." This is not said in denigration of his poetry, but in recognition of a courageous effort to make literature a way of life in parlous times. In some respects, the twenty years at Copse Hill represent an estimable experiment that failed; but, if Hayne produced no really great poetry while there, he at least devoted himself to the profession of letters more single-mindedly and more faithfully than had even Poe or Simms before him. Indeed, few poets of his own generation were willing to commit themselves to such an extent. In this light, Hayne's experience offers invaluable insight into the situation of the Southern artist in nineteenth-century American society; and his example is eminently worthy of examination by both literary historian and critic.

CHAPTER 2

Early Poetry, 1845-65

PAUL Hamilton Hayne began writing verse at an early age (one account claims that he was nine years old), and his audience was his mother and his cousin Susan B. Hayne. Among his efforts are the following titles: "The Violet," "Poor Piggy," "To the Ocean," "Winter," "The Drunkard's Grave," and "Freedom." One notes the conventional romantic themes and is impressed by the early attempt at humor. "Poor Piggy," for example, is a "humble lay" about a "beauteous pig/ Endowed with wisdom supernatural/Inasmuch as it could eat both hominy and rice" whose life is brought to an untimely end by the "butcher's cruel knife." The boy doubtless did not know about Thomas Gray's cat or Philip Freneau's bee, but his pig (if not his poem) is worthy of either.

As his muse developed, young Hayne celebrated the beauties of Carolina and Charleston and gradually addressed himself to political and martial themes. In 1845 he appeared in print for the first time when "The Ashley at the Battery," a poem signed Alpheus, was published on September 11 by the Charleston *Courier*:

> The Ashley flows and glitters on,
> Reflecting all the sunset sky;
> Cool zephyrs from the rippling tide,
> So soft and pure when eve is nigh.
>
> Now, grateful walks adorn thy brink,
> No longer trod by bounding deer;
> But beauty, taste and fashion meet,
> And love the lingering day light here.

The poet then addresses the stream, urges the "sweet Ashley" to "echo" "some legend" from the past and to "sweep in pride and peace." Thus, early in his career Hayne's verse bears certain distinguishing marks. It is smooth and mellifluous; it is conventionally Romantic in idea and diction; and it suggests the influence of earlier poets, in this instance Spenser, Burns, Tennyson, and Poe.

With the approach of the Mexican War, Hayne turned to sterner strains. "Lines—On the Death of Colonel Pierce M. Butler" is dated April 8, 1849; but it commemorates an event of August, 1847, and may have been written earlier. The *Southern Literary Messenger* printed it in the following June. The stanzas quoted below are characteristic of the elegiac quality and chivalric attitude of the whole:

> His gallant sword is firmly grasped—hold! let
> it linger there—
> The spotless blade that Butler bore, another
> must not bear—
> He kept his honour, like the steel—the bright
> steel by his side—
> And only clasped the treasure close—still
> closer—when he died.
>
> . . . .
>
> Cover the pale face of the dead: ere long the
> flowers will bloom,
> And scatter o'er his honoured grave their glory
> and perfume—
> 'Ere long they too will withering lie, like the
> cold dust beneath—
> But 'round his name, the flowers of fame shall
> form a fadeless wreath.

Here is a solemn tribute to a dead knight whose sword is spotless still and whose name will never die. Butler, a former governor of South Carolina and the leader of the Palmetto Regiment, died leading a charge at Churubusco. The view of the slain patriot expressed in "Lines" suggests that of Theodore O'Hara's better-known elegy, "The Bivouac of the Dead," which was written a year later about the same war; "Lines" is interesting now chiefly for this reason and for its anticipation of Hayne's Civil War verse. [1]

During the late 1840's, Hayne began contributing to the *South-ern Literary Gazette*, as well as to the *Southern Literary Mes-senger*. Many of these poems were published pseudonymously (Basil Ormond and the Greek letter Theta are two of his signa-tures), and some were signed P. H. H. The titles frequently sug-gest a turn to the sort of romance and sentiment popular in al-bum or gift-book verse of the day, as in "To ———, On Hearing Her Sing in Public," "Think of Thee!," and "To E., On Receiving a Flower." [2] To his credit, Hayne did not collect these "effusions," but he later reprinted others just as weak and inane.

Much of the verse mentioned thus far seems quite occasional. Indeed, prior to his stint in 1852–53 as associate editor (and later editor) of the *Southern Literary Gazette*, Hayne's verse is that of the dilettante poet or amateur dabbler. Surely this char-acteristic is not strange for one whose work was written when he was in college or studying law. After giving up law in Decem-ber, 1852, and after editing his own journal for a year, his atti-tude toward his poetry became serious enough for him to seek to publish a volume of his verse and to remark that his "heart and soul" were in literature. [3]

I *Poems* (1855)

Hayne's first collection, *Poems* (1855), was published at his expense by Ticknor and Fields, the well-known Boston firm, in November, 1854. A gathering of his early verse from periodicals, it also contains some work written particularly for this book. The longest poem, "The Temptation of Venus," appears for the first time; but others—"Life and Death," "Stanzas. To J. S.," and "A Fragment"—had previously appeared.

Dedicated to his wife (a "gentle Critic"), these miscellaneous "lays" suggest some of Hayne's interests in theme and form and provide a more adequate basis for a judgment of his early work than the juvenilia already discussed. "Aspirations" (later called "The Will and the Wing") announces, in effect, another dedi-cation—the poet's response to "the vision of a life divine":

> To have the will to soar, but not the wings,—
> Eyes fixed forever on a starry height,
> Where stately shapes of grand imaginings
> Flash down the splendors of imperial light;

And yet to lack the charm that makes them ours,
Th' obedient vassals of that conquering spell,
Whose omnipresent and ethereal powers,
Encircle Heaven, nor fear to enter Hell;

This is the doom of Tantalus—the thirst
For beauty's balmy fount to quench the fires
Of the wild passion that our soul hath nurst
In hopeless promptings—unfulfilled desires.

This lyric aptly characterizes Hayne's situation as a poet in 1855 and, for that matter, thirty years later as well. He had the will to soar but not always the wings; his eyes had caught a vision which persuaded him that he must nevertheless devote himself to trying regardless of his gifts.

The "leader" of this volume, to use Hayne's term, is "The Temptation of Venus," subtitled "A Monkish Legend." In a prefatory note Hayne points out what the "early Christian Church" and the followers of Augustine and Chrysostom thought of the Greco-Roman "deification of Love, as exemplified in the conception of Venus" (p. v). "I have endeavored," he explains, anticipating Tennyson's interpretation of the subject in *Idylls of the King*, "to give to the legend a deeper moral significance, to enforce the truth that the apotheosis of the Sense is the funeral of the Soul, and that in the maelstrom of the passions, virtue and happiness are sure to go down together" (p. vi).

This intent he fulfilled in seventy-eight stanzas of six lines each, rhyming *ababcc*. In a narrative sung by an unidentified narrator, a young man named Philemon is reared by monks in a convent in the Egyptian desert not far from the Nile. Though of a noble nature, Philemon strays one day to a "shadowy ruin" where "statues of Grecian gods" "lay half-buried in the drift." There he sees the "Image" of her "Whose empire is the universe of hearts,/ Whose influence, all-pervading and all-seeing,/ Glows, like a golden joy, round Nature's being." And there he returns to worship until he loses his old faith and, "subdued to her command," passes with her "to Love's Elysian-land." Borne on two "milk-white chargers," they enter a wilderness and follow a pathway pervaded by a "rich, voluptuous light" to a palace whose domes and spires fill the sky. The palace is a paradise where thrilling sounds and visions prompt "the desire of further knowledge"; and, in a grotto not unlike the Bower of Bliss at the "most bewitching Hour of all the Hours," Philemon "blindly yields" to the Temptress. Thus sunk in "pestilential pool of Sensual Sin," this "pale prodigal" (now not unlike the Dante of "The Purgatorio") is nevertheless saved by the intervention of an "Image of divine serenity" who, in this light, may stand for the spirit of Beatrice and who tells him, as Beatrice informed Dante in Canto 30, "Thy soul hath lost its God-ward impulse long,/ And thou art dead to Crown, and Palm, and Song." "Look back," she orders him, "and mark the bloom/ That blossomed on thy childhood's golden sky...." The Image's concluding remarks (LXXXVI–LXXXVIII), though there is no way to be sure that Hayne knew the *Divine Comedy* well at this time, also suggest Beatrice's treatment of Dante in the late cantos of "The Purgatorio" and in the final vision of "The Paradiso":

> Go forth to find thy crime's just recompense,
> Go forth to meet the Sorrow and the Shame,
> Which to the Souls who canonize the Sense,
> Cling ever, like fierce Serpents born of Flame,
> Draw in earth's lowest Air thy laboring breath,
> And learn the full significance of death.
>
> Yet from the ruin of thy low estate,
> A penitential patience hath sufficed
> To plume the heart for the Empyreal gate,
> And the serene benignity of Christ;
> In humbleness and prayer work out thy doom,
> Till Glory trembles from the depths of Gloom.
>
> Then may'st thou face the Beautiful, and bare
> Thy willing spirit in the starry sea
> Of still Beatitudes,—then may'st thou share
> Our God's high Noon of Immortality,
> And drink from His grand eyes that burn above,
> The quenchless light and perfect peace of love.

The poem is, to be sure, no masterpiece, nor is it one of Hayne's best. It fails as a narrative for obvious reasons (Hayne himself did not include it in the Complete Edition, but it contains some beautiful stanzas, as, for example, those giving the immediate background and moment of Philemon's fall (LXIV–LXVI).

They reach a grotto, bowered about with vines,
Whence gleam the luscious grapes thro' the dusk rays,
Like sapphire globes of a soft flame, that shrines
The subtle essence the wine-votaries praise,
And there, through bars of deepening verdure glows
A sensuous mystery of divine repose.

The full-orbed Moon is setting in the West,
Flooding the landscape with a Sea of splendor,
The wanton Wind faints on the rose's breast
In delicate dalliance, tremulous and tender,
And a serene and silvery haze is spread
Among the tranquil spaces overhead.

O! most bewitching Hour of all the Hours,
The rugged, common Time is not thy Sire,
Thou stealest forth from the voluptuous flowers,
Born of their passion, and the starry fire
Flushed o'er them, as a God's love bathed of old,
A mortal maid in a rich rain of gold.

The examples of Spenser, Keats, Poe, and Tennyson are evident here; but the young poet has caught some of his masters' magic and made some verbal melody of his own.

The other pieces in the volume—chiefly sonnets and brief lyrics—cover the usual range of subjects in a first book: love, life and death, nature, tolerance, and filial devotion. Two poems on two of these topics deserve mention: "Shelley," a sonnet in defense of the misunderstood poet and thinker, and "My Father," a tribute to a parent Hayne never really knew.

In "Shelley," a young bard generously defends an older brother and scorns those bigots who, "because they thought his doctrines were not just," "wounded the noblest of the sons of God":

The heart's most cherished benefactions riven,
They strove to humble, blacken and malign,
A soul whose charities were wide as Heaven,
Whose *deeds*, if not his *doctrines*, were divine;
And in the name of Him, whose sunshine warms
The evil as the righteous, deemed it good
To wreak their bigotry's relentless storms
On one whose nature was not understood.
Ah! well! God's ways are wondrous,—it may be
His seal hath not been set to man's decree.

Several elements of the so-called Romantic situation may be observed here: the misunderstood poet and the unseeing, ungrateful world, as well as the dichotomy between action and theory ("deeds" and "doctrines"). But a traditional view of God is also offered in the final couplet which suggests a considerable difference of opinion between the two poets in regard to the deity. At the same time, this divergence also underscores Hayne's liberality in judging others of the guild.

The poem on his father, published originally in the *Messenger* for September, 1851, shows Hayne yearning for the parent he hardly knew. He grew up without him: "Never in boyhood have I blithely sprung/ To catch my father's voice, or climb his knee. . . ." Though his father was no hero ("No laurel garland rests upon his tomb"), the poet has "shrined his memory in my mind." From this point, the poem turns to those left behind, the wife and child; and it ends with a prophecy of reunion for all "by the Eternal streams."

Poems was noticed favorably in several important magazines but not so favorably by the reviewer in *Putnam's Monthly* for February, 1855. Faced with the prospect of discussing three "new adventures" in poetry, Hayne's among them, the critic could find little merit in any of the books. He considered Hayne's verse "indistinct in thought, the efflux of mere emotions," and not "studied long enough to have any clearness" nor written "for a clear purpose," especially since he thought the titles of the poems frequently vague and general: "Lines," "Stanzas," "A Fragment."

The reviews in *Harper's New Monthly* and *Graham's Magazine* were much more generous. The writer in *Harper's* for January, 1855, noted the "true poetry" in the volume, liked the versification and imagery, thought well of "several of the smaller poems," and concluded that the work as a whole gave "promise of excellence." In the February *Graham's*, E. P. Whipple characterized the volume as "one of great promise as well as of fine performance." The *Messenger* printed a laudatory account of the volume in the same month, and other notices were encouraging; but Hayne himself knew his limitations. "The volume is not what I could wish it," he wrote his wife from Boston on November 11, 1854, "but I have been told that many of the Poems denote *prom-*

ise & that is all I care for. I will rise yet, dearest, & carry you up with me."

II *Sonnets, and Other Poems* (1857)

Within two years Hayne had another volume of verse ready for the press. Published in Charleston in early February, 1857, this slender sheaf of seventy-two pages was dedicated to Emily Hayne: "First through thy loving lips in youthful days, / The Poets wooed me; first, beside thy knee / Caught I the Poet's rapture, pure and strong." In a prefatory note, he pays his respects to the sonnet as a poetic form. "A successful Sonnet," he asserts, "is among the most unique of imaginative creations." It "addresses itself to the scholar," for it "is too delicate a piece of workmanship, too fine in its adjustment and harmonies to please the ear, or the fancy of the casual reader." But the poet must accept this limitation in audience and maintain with Coleridge that his vocation is its " 'own exceeding great reward.' " Holding such views and knowing also that there was little precedent in American literature, Hayne was either audacious or lacking in judgment in publishing, even in a small printing, a volume of sonnets in 1857.

Moreover, this second volume was not a new edition of Hayne's verse. *Poems* contained eleven sonnets, if the dedicatory one is included; *Sonnets* offers forty-three lyrics in that form, of which six had previously appeared in the first publication. *Sonnets* is then a new gathering of Hayne's work; and, though it does not reveal any particular growth over his earlier effort, it clearly underscores his interest in a type of poetry and presents the evidence of his performance.

In his latest collection, Hayne writes of the old poets, considers his own place among them, notes the seasons, celebrates nature and love, rings the changes on a political theme or two, takes up the mysteries of life and death, and addresses pieces to his wife and new son. If there is not much variety in form (Hayne is partial to the Petrarchan model with some freedom of treatment as regards its "four arbitrary parts"), there is plenty in theme; but the topics are in the main conventional.

What of the poets? Shall only the "great Poets" speak for man? Minor bards must also sing.

> Shall my thought's humble heaven no longer ring
> With pleasant lays, because the empyreal height
> Doth stretch beyond it, lifting to the light
> The Titan pinion of Song's sun-crowned King.
> 'Tis a false thought! the thrush a fitful flight
> Ventures in vernal dawns, a happy note
> Thrills from the russet linnet's gentle throat,
> Though far above the eagle soars in might,
> And the glad skylark—an etherial mote,
> Sings in high realms that mock our straining sight.

Poets should see and record "Summer's past renown" and the coming of October; they should importune their ladies to lift high their thought and "tell the Ariel element to bear/the burden of thy whispered heart to me. . . ." Nature waits to be celebrated:

> . . . Life is born
> From the glad heart of Nature, roused anew
> To pulse in freedom through the deepening blue
> Of tranquil skies, to bend the golden corn
> In broad savannahs, and to stir the sea
> With odorous breezes rippling into calm,
> Where by the still lagoons, the pensive palm
> Doth take the winds' faint kisses languidly . . . .

A political destiny claims the bard's attention. The conflict between the sections offers no opportunity for a "Patriot" to falter. Duty, honor, pride, manhood demand in this "righteous quarrel" that "we shall stand full-sized in Freedom's light." If defeat comes and "Wrong conquers Right," it should provide further food for an examination of the mystery of life:

> Why fainteth Love in the rude grasp of Hate?
> Why creeps the Genius which hath wings to soar?
> And human Misery fronting human Fate,
> Scorn and deny Thee, Father, evermore?

The answer comes in the revelation of death:

> "Light give me light!"—the expiring Poet cried,
> Closing his languid eyelids on the day,
> And with that solemn cry he passed away;
> And haply Doubt was solved, and Error died,
> And glimmering Trust was grandly glorified,
> Even in the moment of his mightiest need . . . .

Or: "There is no death but change, soul claspeth soul,/And all are portion of the Immortal whole."

Two of Hayne's most interesting and revealing sonnets deal with his newborn son and his study. The first of these (later called "To W. H. H.") is addressed to William Hamilton Hayne, his first and only child, who had been born on March 11, 1856. In September, Hayne expressed his pleasure to R. H. Stoddard: "I too can boast of a son, a six monther who has just cut his first teeth, an olive complexioned, black eyed, lively little scoundrel, the light and joy of the household ..." (*Letters*, 16). This joy and the dream of a son following in his father's footsteps animate Hayne's sonnet:

> I pray the Angel in whose hands the sum
> Of mortal fates in mystic darkness lies,
> That to the soul which fills these deepening eyes,
> Sun-crowned and clear, the SPIRIT OF SONG may come;
> That strong-winged Fancies, with melodious hum
> Of pluméd vans, may touch to sweet surprise
> His poet nature, born to glow and rise,
> And thrill to worship though the world be dumb;
> That Love, and Will, and Genius, all may blend
> To make His soul a guiding star of Time,
> True to the purest thought, the noblest end,
> Full of all richness, gentle, wise, complete,
> In whose still heights, and most ethereal clime,
> Beauty, and Faith, and plastic Passion meet.

"My Study" summarizes well Hayne's general attitude toward the worlds of action and of books. It suggests that the poet's whole life was of a piece. Before the Civil War, he managed to get by on his own or his family's resources and was not involved in "Mammon conflicts crowned by Fraud or Chance." After the war, he retreated to Copse Hill; and, though he was forced to work for his bread, he lived away from the "present strife" of the world. The poem aptly characterizes his romantic, bookish nature. He was not, as had been his father and his Uncle Robert, a man of action. He was rather one who sought "the fields of quiet Arcadies" and gloried in "the gorgeous vistas of Romance":

> This is my world! within these narrow walls,
> I own a princely service; the hot care

And tumult of our frenzied life are here,
But as a ghost, and echo; what befalls
In the far mart to me is less than nought;
I walk the fields of quiet Arcadies,
And wander by the brink of hoary seas,
Calmed to the tendance of untroubled Thought:
Or if a livelier humor should enhance
The slow-timed pulse, 'tis not for present strife,
The sordid zeal with which our Age is rife,
Its Mammon conflicts crowned by Fraud or Chance,—
But gleamings of the lost, heroic life,
Flushed through the gorgeous vistas of Romance.

Of the longer poems in this collection, mention may be made of "Ode to Sleep." The spokesman in this lyric addresses the "Serenest Angel—Sleep," urges it to "cloud" his spirit with a "sweet eclipse," asks for "Oblivion's balsam," a "nepenthe" of forgetfulness, and an "Elysium of release" so that he may be borne to a "noiseless Land" and stand "Close on a duskier country, and more grand/Mysterious solitude than thine, O, Sleep!" Then, he may "pass gently" from the sleep of life to the more lasting sleep of death. In the final passage of the ode, Sleep steals "like an incantation on the soul," and the speaker yearns for the "diviner sleep" of "sacred Death":

Then woo me here amid these flowery charms;
Breathe on my eyelide; press thy odorous lips
Close to mine own; enfold me in thine arms,
And cloud my spirit with thy sweet eclipse;
And while from waning depth to depth I fall,
Down-lapsing to the utmost depth of all—
Till wan Forgetfulness, obscurely stealing,
Creeps like an Incantation on the soul,
And o'er the slow ebb of my conscious life
Dies the thin flush of the last conscious feeling,
And, like abortive thunder, the dull roll
Of sullen passions swells,—far, far away,—
O, Angel! loose the chords which cling to strife,
Sever the gossamer bondage of my breath—
And let me pass gently, as winds in May,
From the dim realm which owns thy shadowy sway,
To THY diviner sleep, O, sacred Death!

This death is hardly the sane and sacred one that Whitman writes about, but the gradual dissolution of life in its progress through the "waning depths" of sleep to the divine domain of death is effectively traced and evoked. And the tranquil tone and air of quiet acceptance contribute to the creation of a mood and music seldom present in Hayne's early poetry.

The reception of *Sonnets* was meager. The Charleston newspapers "puffed" the volume, as Hayne was pleased to note; but few notices appeared in Northern periodicals for the simple reason that review copies were scarce. John R. Thompson greeted the book with a sonnet of his own, but he had no copy of it and was forced to base his critical comments in the *Messenger* for March, 1857, on "copious extracts" from Charleston newspapers.

The most favorable review appeared in the *Home Journal,* a New York weekly edited by N. P. Willis to which Hayne contributed; and it was written by Stoddard after he had received a personal copy from Hayne. Stoddard considered the work in the collection "thoughtful and earnest and often highly felicitous." He was impressed by the "finish" imparted to the poems, and he especially liked the sonnets: "we consider them among the very best ever written in this country. . . . With the exception of Mr. Boker, no American poet at all approaches Mr. Hayne in this difficult school of poetry." He concluded that Hayne had now "placed himself in the front rank of southern authors." This was high praise from Stoddard, a man noted neither for wearing his heart on his sleeve nor for promoting the books of his friends. Yet this view is too generous, then or now; the public, however, was less responsive, and only about two hundred copies of the three hundred issued were sold, as Hayne informed Stoddard on August 28, 1859 (*Letters,* 35). It is entirely possible, of course, that the poet stopped the sale of this volume, for it was published at his own expense and he remarks in his preface to *Avolio* (1860) that the small edition of *Sonnets* was "partially suppressed."

Whatever the reason, the book received little attention; and, though Hayne had anticipated such a reception in his dedicatory sonnet—"Who dares to touch this small Lyre, / Sings for his own deep heart, not others' praise"—he was disheartened and disappointed, but he wasted little time in reproaching himself or oth-

ers, preferring instead to get his poems written so that he could
publish another collection.

III   *Avolio* (1859)

This policy resulted two years later in the publication of
Avolio, a book containing the best poems Hayne wrote prior to
the Civil War. Unlike *Sonnets*, it is, in a sense, a collected edition
of his work to date. A careful selection of poems from the first
two volumes is included, and a number of new poems are added.
The offering is much more varied than before: the reader may
choose from among narratives, odes, sonnets, brief lyrics and
songs, dramatic sketches, and fugitive verses.

The volume is dedicated in a sonnet to E. P. Whipple whose
friendship has survived "long dreary years" as well as "Distance
and Fate." Whipple's powers as a critic of the "greatest Seers"
and the "humbler bards" are lauded. A plea for forgiveness for
anything "false or feeble" is entered for the present collection.
"Whatever its artistic, or poetical imperfections," Hayne wrote
Whipple when he sent him a copy of the sonnet on September
10, 1859, the poem is "an expression of sincere & earnest feeling"
(*Letters*, 64).

The chief poem in the collection, "Avolio," appeared first in
Russell's Magazine for April, 1859, and follows the fashion Hayne
had established earlier in "The Temptation of Venus." A narrative
of over four hundred lines, it is based with some "expansion" and
with an interpretation "more purely ideal," as Hayne writes in
his preface, upon a "story contained in that most charming of
recent Essayical and Legendary Miscellanies, 'The Indicator,' by
Leigh Hunt." Compounded of elements from the characters of
the books of knight errantry and of the Romantic epic (Tasso's
Tancred appears near the end), from the Tennysonian Lotos-
land atmosphere, and from hints and suggestions of verbal melody from Spenser and Keats, to say nothing of its gift from Hunt,
"Avolio" derives its nourishment primarily from Hayne's masters
and poetic forebears.

Avolio, a Florentine gentleman "self-exiled from his country"
and skilled in the lore of arms and chivalry, loves adventure
and burns to "vanquish" strange foes and "rescue maidens from

malignant spells." Having been borne on an "enchanted" voyage
to an island paradise, Avolio "challenges" his peers and the
ship's company to "explore the solitudes" and conquer "this flowery empire." A "motley band" follows him into "the wood's deep
places" to a "sombre mound . . . planted thick with dark funereal
trees." There "the whole preternatural landscape dawns/Freez-
ingly on them," and the "affrighted crew," which flees inconti-
nently, leaves Avolio to hear the "ghostly din" of hounds and
horns and the "wizard chase" of a dreamlike reproduction of the
death of Actaeon. He reaches a fount and then a rivulet amidst
Poesque surroundings "with dank dark alders set,/Blurred in its
turbid tides the o'erhanging sky;/The melancholy waters seemed
to sigh/In wailful murmurs of articulate woe. . . ."

He hears the "Song of the Imprisoned Naiad." This sad ballad
contrasts in form and in point of view with the iambic couplets of
the narrative preceding and following it. A legend describing
Diana's jealousy and authority, it tells in the words of the Naiad
of her separation by Diana from her Oread lover, of her "oblivion" in the "sullen depths," and of her grief which "knows not an
autumn blight."

"His reason in a whirling chaos lost" at such "heart-melting
music," Avolio sees a "sombrous mansion" with "Long wreaths
of ghostly ivy on its walls." Then a serpent, which takes shape
before his horrified eyes, announces itself as Cos's "fated Queen"
who had "cursed the great Diana" and who is doomed to remain
a monster until rescued by a man willing to kiss her "on the
mouth." The knight is reluctant, but, when the serpent saves two
hares from a "threatening falcon," he performs the "deed" and
discovers to his "rapture" that the hideous thing has become a
maiden "Fair as the tropic morn, when morn is new." Pledging
themselves to each other, Avolio and his bride shed a beneficent
influence on Cos. When word of this "most strange event"
reaches the world, many knights come to visit the island, Tancred
among them. Concerned that pagan influences on the lady might
still be strong, Tancred asks whether she still worships Diana.
Avolio instantly replies that she reveres only Christ the Lord, and
the lady without a word looks with "modest passion" on her
knightly savior "as one who longed to whisper tenderly,/O! brave,
kind Heart! I worship only thee!'"

In some respects Hayne has improved on his source. He has,

for example, introduced the death of Actaeon and the song of the Naiad to suggest Diana's authority and a precedent for the queen's punishment. Furthermore, he has concentrated on the knightly character of Avolio so as to provide him a better motivation for overcoming his repugnance and doing the deed. And he has undertaken to describe the island in lush and elaborate terms. In these ways he has added to Hunt's account of "The Daughter of Hippocrates" in the *Indicator*.

Regardless of these improvements (there are others that he might have made but did not), the narrative is rather weak even as a legend. Its ancient and medieval elements are unassimilated, and the relationship between pagan and Christian views is never resolved. Hayne handles the verse form adequately enough. Few of the couplets seem strained, and the paragraph structure suits the movement of the story. Chaucer's example has served well here, as perhaps in the Loathly Lady theme, though Hayne also had in mind Keats's "Lamia." The diction and atmosphere, however, seem as derivative as the source material; for Spenser, Keats, Tennyson, and Poe may all be heard from time to time. The result is that the poem seems bookish and imitative, and the poet's own personality and spirit are completely lacking. "Avolio" suggests that Hayne does not always make his own what he has appropriated from his predecessors and contemporaries. [4]

The other types of poems in the collection may be treated more briefly. In the odes, conventional in form and topic, each speaker is heard expressing feelings or announcing opinions. The "Ode Delivered on the First Anniversary of the Carolina Art Association" holds forth on the worlds of action and thought, of science and art. [5] Science "delves" into and "explores" the land, sea, universe, and even man; but it has failed to find man's "spirit." Her "beauteous sister" brings a "nobler message" from the "mighty Masters"—the sculptors, painters, and poets. Homer, Aeschylus, Shakespeare, Michelangelo, and Raphael, those who fashioned the "concrete forms of Beauty and of Power," pass in review before great altars "upreared" to love, beauty, grandeur, truth, and "all things wise and pure."

The other long lyric, "Nature the Consoler. An Ode," which had appeared first in the *Southern Literary Messenger* for October, 1858, is reminiscent of Wordsworth's ideas about nature and its beneficent influence on the poet until, in the final section, a plea is offered for ultimate transition to a "sphere" where mortals assume immortality. In this stanza, echoing the Tennyson of "Ulysses" and the Poe of "Israfel," Hayne anticipates some of the ideas, imagery, and diction of parts of "Passage to India" and "The Marshes of Glynn":

> Soothed by this milder glory, let us pass
> To the weird land of peace-embosomed dreams,
> The lapsing of the far-off forest streams
> 　　　Rustling the reedy grass,
> Will make rare music for us, till we reach
> 　　　The mystic beach,
> The margin of the starry sea of sleep;
> Thence, launching on the waters, let us sail
> Beneath a Heaven of ever-living blue,
> Thronged with fair loving faces, fair though pale,
> The faces of the faithful souls we knew
> In our glad youth, before the death-clouds lowered;—
> O! let us hold them in communion deep.
> And learn, although our lower world is fair,
> 　　　*A lovelier sphere,*
> *Circled by sunlights of more gorgeous dye,*
> *And gifted with an ampler wealth of flowers,*
> *Dwells in the unimagined heights of Air,*
> *Unmeasured by dull Time, the weary-houred,—*
> And further learn, *that* world shall yet be ours,
> Wherein, released from every human care,
> The Mortal puts on Immortality! [6]

The shorter poems include some of the best sonnets from among those published in the first two volumes, as well as such lyrics as "The Island in the South," "The Eve of the Bridal," "My Father" (cut to its advantage from the first version in *Poems*), "The Realm of Rest," and "The Will, and the Wing" (called "Aspirations" in *Poems*). The new lyrics treat some of the same themes—love, nature, myth—of the earlier pieces. "Bought and Sold" seems to anticipate a view of the female in modern society expressed by Lanier in "The Symphony": "For a woman, a woman, that's bought and sold/ In a mart where the Devil pays down the gold,/ Goes forth from the sacred door!" "The Two Summers" points out that the soul has an Indian summer as surely as does the fall of the year, and asserts that it is the season to die "while Peace and Sunshine rule the cloudless West." "Lethe" describes the river and the region made famous by Homer and Virgil, where "all things droop in slumber" and "even the sluggish River's flow/ Sounds like the dying surges of the sea/ To ears far inland."

Altogether, *Avolio* is an advance beyond the earlier volumes in both variety and performance; nevertheless, the collection promises rather than fulfills—points the critics were not slow to make. Whipple in his review in the *Evening Transcript* maintained that there was "hardly a poem . . . which did not convey a sense of the writer's intellectual growth." Lowell's notice in the *Atlantic Monthly* for January, 1860, also notes this progress:

There is a great deal of real poetic feeling and expression in this volume, and, we think, the hope of better things to come. . . . The volume would have gained in quality by losing in quantity, but to give too much is the mistake of all young writers, and it is, perhaps, only by making it once for themselves that they can learn to sift. . . .

But, after all, it seems to us that Mr. Hayne has the root of the matter in him; and we shall look to meet him again, bringing a thinner, yet a fuller book. The present volume shows thoughtfulness, culture, sensibility to natural beauty, and great refinement of feeling. . . . [He] need only persevere in self-culture to be able to produce poems that shall win for him a national reputation.[7]

Though Lowell apparently considers Hayne a younger man in age and experience than he actually was, his general criticism is not only "indulgent & kindly," as Hayne himself characterized it, but just and accurate. Despite his age and experience (he was almost thirty and *Avolio* was his third book) and despite the obvious improvement in his work, Hayne's muse did not develop rapidly; and his latest volume shows no marked advance in terms of ideas, thought, or feeling. Yet his talent might have found fruition soon had the Civil War not intervened.

IV   *Civil War Poetry*

Hayne's war verses are for the most part fugitive and uncollected. He planned, so he wrote John R. Thompson in 1867, to publish a volume of "War-Poems" and dedicate it to Thompson, but he could not find a publisher. He later included several war pieces in *Legends and Lyrics* (1872) and collected seventeen titles in the Complete Edition (1882). [8]

The Confederate cause was right so far as Hayne was concerned; and, though he began to have some doubt about victory as early as February, 1862, he faithfully supported his "beloved country" with every means at his disposal until the end. His chief weapon, of course, was his pen.

The themes of Hayne's martial songs are varied but conventional. Thus he sings of Carolina in "My Mother-Land," "Charleston," "Battle of Charleston Harbor," "Charleston at the Close of 1863," and other pieces; of the military leaders in "Stuart," "The Kentucky Partisan," and "Stonewall Jackson"; of the soldiers in "The Substitute," "Beyond the Potomac," and "Our Martyrs"; of the sacrifice of the people in "Beauregard's Appeal"; of the great engagements in "Vicksburg"; and of the enemy in "Butler's Proclamation." [9]

His views of the justness of the Southern cause are clearly outlined in "My Mother-Land," and he offered them as the voice of the people:

> Our course is righteous, and our aims are just!
> Behold, we seek
> Not merely to preserve for noble wives
> The virtuous pride of unpolluted lives,
> To shield our daughters from the servile hand,
> And leave our sons their heirloom of command,
> In generous perpetuity of trust;
> Not only to defend those ancient laws,
> Which Saxon sturdiness and Norman fire
> Welded forevermore with freedom's cause,
> And handed scathless down from sire to sire—
> Nor yet our grand religion, and our Christ,
> Unsoiled by secular hates, or sordid harms,
> (Though these had sure sufficed
> To urge the feeblest Sybarite to arms)—
> But more than all, because embracing all,
> Ensuring all, self-government, the boon
> Our patriot statesmen strove to win and keep. . . . [10]

In "Charleston!" (*Mercury*, May 8, 1862), he celebrates his native city, the "warrior Queen of Ocean," and exhorts her to stand firm when the "war-tornado blows"; but

> If strength, and will, and courage fail
> > To cope with ruthless numbers,
> And thou must bend, despairing, pale,
> > Where thy last hero slumbers,
> Lift the red torch, and light the fire
> > Amid those corpses gory,
> And on thy self-made funeral pyre,
> > Pass from the world to glory.

He reveres the moral stature of Stonewall Jackson: "We bow before this grandeur of the spirit;/ We worship, and adore/ God's image burning through it evermore. . . ." He admires the courage and daring of J. E. B. Stuart ("his very name/ Embodies a thought of fire") and "gallant Morgan" ("God! who would not gladly die/ Beside that glorious man"), and an uncollected poem entitled "The Kentucky Partisan" (*Southern Literary Messenger*, April, 1862) reveals Hayne's respect for the leader as well as his hatred for the foe. For "our ruined homesteads," "our women outraged," and "our ravaged land," John Hunt Morgan "has sworn (and recks not/ Who may cross his path)—/ That the foe shall feel him/ In his torrid wrath."

Confederate soldiers are no less dauntless in battle than their generals: for, like the men of Lee in Maryland in September, 1862, they are "giants of courage" and "Anaks in fight," and they will topple the tyrant, according to the poet in "Beyond the Potomac":

> 'Neath a blow swift and mighty the tyrant may fall;
> Vain, vain! to his gods swells a desolate call;
> Hath his grave not been hollowed, and woven his pall,
> Since they passed o'er the river?

A few years after the war, Whittier wrote Hayne that "Beyond the Potomac" was "one of the few *real* poems produced on your side by the war" and ranked it with J. R. Randall's "Maryland, My Maryland," Timrod's war poems, and J. W. Palmer's "Stonewall Jackson's Way." "Of course," he concluded, "we did not like the *sentiment* of these poems, but we knew their true poetic ring." [11]

The note of sacrifice is not absent in Hayne's poems. When General Beauregard addressed an appeal to the planters of the

Mississippi Valley in March, 1862, for plantation bells to be melt-
ed into cannon, some churches offered their bells; and Hayne
supported the idea wholeheartedly in "Beauregard's Appeal":

> Yea! since the need is bitter
> Take down those sacred bells,
> Whose music speaks of hallowed joys,
> And passionate farewells!

With a "people's ALL at stake," surely this gift, the speaker in
the poem maintains, is no "desecration." The people must crush
their "struggling sorrow" and sacrifice "the bells from a hundred
spires," for

> A cause like ours is holy,
> And it useth holy things;
> While over the storm of a righteous strife,
> May shine the angel's wings.

> Where'er our duty leads us,
> The grace of God is there,
> And the lurid shrine of war may hold
> The Eucharist of prayer.[12]

Of the actual fighting which attracted Hayne's muse, the contest for Vicksburg elicited one of his best efforts on the war and,
surely, one of the most widely anthologized of all his poems,
"Vicksburg.—A Ballad." Dedicated with "respect and admiration
to Gen. Earl Van Dorn," the "grand young leader" referred to in
the first stanza, and dated August 6, 1862, this piece appeared in
the Charleston *Daily Courier* for January 1, 1863. The poem also
celebrates the courage of the civilians, especially of women and
children, in the midst of the long, heavy bombardment of May
18 to July 26, 1862, when Farragut's ships from below and a
squadron of gunboats and rams from above subjected the city to
an intense, intermittent shelling for over two months. When the
bombardment failed to reduce the city's defenses and when the
Arkansas, a makeshift Confederate ironclad, attacked the Federal
fleet in July, Farragut steamed south, and Vicksburg was relieved
until General Grant laid siege a year later and finally forced its
capitulation on July 4, 1863:

> For sixty days and upwards,
> > A storm of shell and shot
> Rained round us in a flaming shower,
> > But still we faltered not.

Despite a "hissing tumult" and a "tempest" of "huge bombs," the "Lord, our shield, was with us," and women "walked the streets" and children played at their "sports":

> Yet the hailing bolts fell faster,
> > From scores of flame-clad ships,
> And about us, denser, darker,
> > Grew the conflict's wild eclipse,
> Till a solid cloud closed o'er us,
>
> . . . .
>
> But the unseen hands of angels
> > Those death-shafts warned aside,
> And the dove of heavenly mercy
> > Ruled o'er the battle tide;
> In the houses ceased the wailing,
> > And through the war-scarred marts
> The people strode, with step of hope,
> > To the music in their hearts.[13]

Hayne, who often characterized the enemy as "Northmen," "foemen," "ruffians," "robbers," and "invaders," could, on occasion, wax eloquent on the subject of Federal depredation and despotism. His rhetorical dander is aroused in "Butler's Proclamation," a rejoinder to General Butler's famous order of May, 1862, regarding the punishment of women who insulted Union officers or soldiers:

> Aye! drop the treacherous mask! throw by
> > The cloak, which veils thine instincts fell,
> Stand forth thou base, incarnate Lie,
> > Stamped with the signet brand of Hell!
> At last we view thee as thou art,
> A trickster with a Demon's heart.

Exhorting his "comrades," as "husbands, brothers, sires," to defend their women, the speaker urges them to "strike home" with "ruthless sword and will." For the perpetrator of this order, there remains but one fate: "For *him*, swift cord! felon grave":

> As loathsome charnel vapors melt
> > Swept by invisible winds to nought,
> So may this Fiend of lust and guilt
> > Die like a nightmare's hideous thought!
> Nought left to mark the monster's name
> > Save—immortality of shame! [14]

Hayne was not an important war poet in the sense that his best verse belongs in the first order of Civil War poetry. He was quite aware that such work was not in his line, and he was eager to yield the palm to Timrod as "the So. Poet of the war." For what had Hayne written in behalf of the Confederacy or on the war that he could hold up to Timrod's "Carolina" or "Spring," or, for that matter, to "Ethnogenesis" or "The Cotton Boll," poems developing larger themes than battles or campaigns? But Hayne's efforts were far from being despised by other Southerners, for he frequently received notes of thanks and congratulation from men in the field—General Beauregard wrote him several times—who wished to let him know that his work in behalf of the cause was appreciated. When Hayne's ballad on Stuart appeared in the *Southern Illustrated News* for November 30, 1862, the editors remarked: "Long may the gallant Stuart live to wield his sabre in defense of Southern rights, and may he always have a Paul Hayne to extol, in beautiful verse, his dauntless courage and his virtues."

As a whole, the poetry that Hayne wrote prior to the end of the Civil War is sentimental and conventional, and it is frequently marred (for modern tastes, at least) by some of the worst aspects of a weak Romanticism in diction, imagery, and point of view. Hayne, who was aware of some of these faults, made sincere efforts to return to Chaucer and other older English poets for nurture and sustenance; but the war put a temporary stop to this development. He managed to read widely at times and to compose in 1864 several drafts of what later became "The Wife of Brittany," one of his best long narratives, but the war was unsettling and distracting. "When one is knocked about as I was, deprived of all tranquility," he explained to Stoddard in a letter

of July 1, 1866, "how *can* one compose properly, or artistically?"
And the conflict itself was distasteful to him. War, he wrote years
later, "cultivates no doubt some marked heroic virtues; but this
one advantage is fearfully counterbalanced by its brutalities, its
woe, its sufferings, so often inflicted upon others; I mean upon
the poor women & children who stay at home." [15] If the war
ended disastrously for Hayne, he could at least look forward to
a time when he might devote himself wholeheartedly to
literature.

CHAPTER 3

Legends and Lyrics, 1872

IN 1864 Hayne made a selection from his poems, and, in the summer of that year, he put the package on a steamer headed for Liverpool; however, Hayne's book presumably failed to arrive in England.[1] After the war he continued to plan to bring out a new collection of his verse. In answer to a query about his "Literary projects" from his old friend John Esten Cooke, the Virginia romancer, Hayne wrote on July 24, 1866, that he had a "goodly pile of MSS. (with *one* long poem to head them), which (God willing), I trust to publish—whenever the chance occurs. A somewhat indefinite hope," he added, "but still—a hope!" (*Letters*, 90).

Less than a year later, as he informed Thompson on March 17, 1867, he hoped "to publish *two* vols, *one* of 'War-Poems,' & the *other* of miscellaneous verses, *chiefly ideal*" (*Letters*, 131). But he could not find a publisher. Though there were one or two exceptions, Northern publishers were reluctant to publish poems lauding the Confederate cause; and those firms willing to bring out Hayne's other poems were chary of taking the usual risks of publication without a substantial subsidy from the poet. Several houses declined his proposals; but, finally, J. B. Lippincott of Philadelphia agreed in the late summer of 1871 to bring out a volume of his verse if Hayne assumed the initial expense of publication. The profits, if any, were to be shared. With the help of his mother, the necessary funds were provided; and *Legends and Lyrics* appeared on January 9, 1872. Copies were soon in the hands of Longfellow, Whittier, Holmes, Howells, Taylor, Lanier, Mrs. Preston, and others, including the reviewers.[2]

The new collection, like his first one, is dedicated to his wife, the "dear Heart" who has shown him that love is more lasting than a "Poet's name"; after all, "even Shakspeare's fame at last shall sink," but "such love as ours, I think,/ Was born, o'er Time and Death to drink/ Of immortality!" Nor is his mother neglected, for the last poem in the volume is addressed to her in acknowledgment of her faith in his "song"; "To thee, as once my earliest rhyme,/ Lo! now, I bring—my latest!"

Only one poem from his previous books—"Ode to Sleep"— is included in *Legends and Lyrics;* otherwise the pieces are new, and the types are varied. The legends are incorporated in several narratives—"Daphles," "The Wife of Brittany," "Cambyses and the Macrobian Bow," and "The Story of Glaucus the Thessalian" —and the lyrics in an elegy written to the memory of Timrod; in pieces addressed to his wife, mother, and son; in several poems assessing his own situation; in three selections from his war verse; in a number of sonnets; and in some miscellaneous items.

I *"The Wife of Brittany"*

The most ambitious poem in the volume is "The Wife of Brittany," a treatment of the "Franklin's Tale" in the *Canterbury Tales.* Written in the spring and summer of 1864, revised from time to time, and published in the *New Eclectic,* a Baltimore monthly, in November, 1870, the narrative, as Hayne always maintained, is "no mere modernization of Chaucer. Excepting the plot," he wrote Edward Spencer, a Maryland journalist and critic, on March 6, 1872, "it has indeed little to do with Chaucer; the few lines retained from the antique verse being in themselves by no means characteristic. What I intended," he explained, "was to embody the old legend—which struck my fancy strangely, despite its grotesquerie—in verse partaking, in some measure, of Dryden's stately 'heroics,' mingled with the freer metrical movement of Keats; taking care to bring the entire story to the reader's view in a series of pictures." [3]

Despite this claim, "The Wife of Brittany" is, as E. W. Parks has shown, not quite so original as Hayne asserted; nor is it, on the other hand, a slavish imitation of the Chaucerian work. [4] Its 909 lines make it one of the longest poems Hayne ever wrote, and the graceful handling of the meter and of materials congenial to his talents make it one of his best.

Though the poem is clearly marked—"(Suggested by the

Frankeleine's Tale of Chaucer.)"—Hayne makes certain basic
changes in Chaucer's treatment of the material, including the
dropping of the role of the Franklin in the narrative by which
stratagem he assumes the role of narrator himself. The poem is
divided into a proem, three parts, and a brief epiloguelike statement at the end.

The proem presents the general purpose ("Truth wed to beauty in an antique tale"), acknowledgment of the poet's debt to
the "old world song" of "tuneful Chaucer," and concludes by an
address and half-apology to the "brave old poet":

> Sustain me, cherish and around me fold
> Thine own hale, sun-warm atmosphere of song,
> Lest I who touch thy numbers, do thee wrong;
> Speed the deep measure, make the meaning shine
> Ruddy and high with healthful spirit wine,
> Till to attempered sense and quickening ears
> My strain some faint harmonious echo bears
> From that rich realm wherein thy cordial art
> Throbbed with its pulse of fire 'gainst youthful
>   England's heart.

The story proper is divided into three parts (or "cantos," as
Hayne sometimes refers to them). The first section deals with
the love and marriage of Arviragus and Iolene (Chaucer's lovers
are called Arveragus and Dorigen), Arviragus' quest for fame in
England, Aurelian's (Chaucer's Squire Aurelius) obsession for
Iolene, and Iolene's plan to teach Aurelian how hopeless his love
is. The second canto is devoted to Aurelian who, in turn, hears
from his brother about a "shrewd clerk-in-law" in Orleans; and
he seeks out the scholar, Artevall, who with "strange spells"
apparently disposes of the rocks on the Breton shore. In the third
part both Arviragus and Aurelian return. Iolene is put to the test
when Aurelian claims her "promise." Arviragus is angry and piti-
less and sees no way to avoid the oath. When she goes to Aurelian, he sees her sad plight, and his "guardian genius" leads him
compassionately to release her from her word. And so, without
disgrace, she returns to her husband and they live thereafter as
"One will, one mind, one joy-encircled fate,/ And one winged
faith that soars beyond the heavenly gate." But Hayne is not content to leave it there:

And now 'tis ended: long, yea, long ago,
Lost on the wings of all the winds that blow,
The dust of these dead loves hath passed away;
Still, still, methinks, a soft, ethereal ray
Illumes the tender record, and makes bright
Its heart-deep pathos with a marvellous light,
So that whate'er of frenzied grief and pain
Marred the pure currents of the crystal strain,
Transfigured shines through fancy's mellowing trance,
Touching with golden haze the quaint old-world romance.

The minor changes Hayne made in his source are numerous, but the major ones, though fewer, are more revealing. Iolene, for example, proposes that the squire remove the rocks not in "pley" as in Chaucer, but in the hope that Aurelian will realize how impossible his passion for her is. In this way, Iolene seems more sympathetic than Dorigen; and her motives are more humane, though her punishment may seem disproportionate. As Parks points out, Aurelian is similar to Aurelius in his "spiritual sickness," but Hayne omits much of the astrological lore and conventional material incidental to the squire's love and the magician's power. The problem of making the rocks disappear is solved in a simple and direct way. The narrator states that Artevall's "strange spells a marvel wrought/ Beyond the utmost reach of credulous thought." The shore becomes to the sight a "wide unwrinkled strand,/ Smooth as thy lovely lady's delicate hand." Both Dorigen and Iolene lament their respective positions and contemplate suicide, but Dorigen summons up the memories of many ladies who chose death rather than a life of dishonor, whereas Iolene is restrained from taking her life by a "mystic voice" which saves her but leaves her distraught and full of anguish. The responses of the husbands are representative of the poets and the times. Arviragus is much angrier and more reproachful, though both knights agree that their wives must keep their pledges. Each squire releases his lady from her promise, but Aurelius does it as a "gentil dede" appropriate to his calling, whereas Aurelian is prompted by what Parks calls a "noble religious impulse."

Altogether, Hayne's changes discard much of the medieval material regarding astrology, magic, and courtly love; the result is a gain in narrative unity. His poem does lose some of the texture and complexity of Chaucer's tale, and "The Wife of Brittany" thereby becomes more Hayne's own than might otherwise have been the case. For, as Parks decides, the "work is an adaptation or redaction, not simply a re-telling of the old tale in modern verse" (115). Of course, by going to Chaucer at all, Hayne ran the risk of critical censure for dealing with matters which were archaic and out-of-date and with materials which had been definitively treated; but he lived in a day when poets on both sides of the Atlantic turned to the medieval past for inspiration and substance. Tennyson's *Idylls of the King* (1842–85), Morris' *Defence of Guenevere* (1858) and *Earthly Paradise* (1868–70), Arnold's *Tristram and Iseult* (1852), Lowell's *The Vision of Sir Launfal* (1848), and Longfellow's *Golden Legend* (1851) and his translation of Dante's *Comedy* (1867) come readily to mind. If Hayne did not equal his master, his adaptation as Parks concludes, possesses "some excellence" and "has much to commend it." A competently handled and lively nineteenth-century narrative poem in the heroic measure, derivative in nature and style, it is worthy of consideration as a modern Romantic treatment of a typical medieval problem.

Though the general critical response was favorable, William Dean Howells and Sidney Lanier found fault with certain aspects of "The Wife of Brittany." In his review in the *Atlantic* for April, 1872, Howells stressed Hayne's supposed indebtedness to William Morris:

To find Mr. Hayne, who has a distinct note of his own, emulating Mr. William Morris . . . is a little curious, for Mr. Hayne is a poet of no recent repute, and Mr. Morris is a passing poetical fashion. . . . Because "Daphles" and "The Wife of Brittany" strongly suggest Mr. Morris's rhymed stories, we cannot praise them, though they have fineness and excellences that belong to Mr. Hayne. They form nearly a third part of his volume, in which, however, there is enough of his own in manner as well as substance abundantly to redeem it. In fact, but for this cant Morrisward in the two poems named, it attests its author's right to be as vigorously as any book of verse that we have lately read.

Howells was wrong about Morris' influence, at least in part because Hayne failed to provide in *Legends and Lyrics* dates of composition for the two poems or to note that he had completed "The Wife of Brittany" and written much of "Daphles" before

Earthly Paradise had been published in America. The *Atlantic* review, however, prompted Hayne to send Howells the full details of composition, and Howells admitted in the May issue that he had been unjust. Hayne was satisfied momentarily; he wrote Mrs. Preston on May 19 that the magazine had "absolutely been guilty of a piece of *pure justice*."

But the matter was not closed. Lanier touched on the question in the *Southern Magazine* for January, 1875, and Hayne acknowledged to Mrs. Preston on January 25 that he did not "particularly like" to have the "charge . . . even *insinuated* again at this late date." Lanier's chief criticism, however, was reserved for another aspect of the poem. Though he had written Hayne on December 8, 1870, that he could not "candidly or uncandidly" criticize "The Wife of Brittany" because he loved it, he described readily enough in 1875 the dangers inherent in reworking old materials: "the plot is only conceivable as a thing of the past, it belongs to the curiosities of history. . . . In the *Wife of Brittany* and in all similar artistic ventures Mr. Hayne will write under the disadvantage of feeling at the bottom of his heart that the passion of the poem is amateur passion, the terror of it amateur terror, and the whole business little more than a dainty titillation of the unreal." [5]

The objections of Howells and Lanier notwithstanding, other literati thought well of "The Wife of Brittany." John R. Thompson offered to send a copy to his friend Tennyson, and Bayard Taylor concluded after reading the poem that "metrical story-telling" was Hayne's "true field." Francis James Child, the Harvard Chaucerian and collector of ballads, generously characterized the poet's accomplishment: "You have made the story your own, much as Chaucer did his originals, and have retold it with great sweetness and tenderness."

The most encouraging criticism, especially in regard to the comparison with Morris, came from E. P. Whipple who not only commended the narrative itself but maintained that it was in some ways superior to similar pieces by Morris. "I have read your poem with great interest and delight," he wrote Hayne on November 8, 1870. "Why should it not be celebrated, like the poems of Morris?" A few months later in Whipple's review of *Legends and Lyrics* he was even more forthright about "Daphles," "Cambyses and the Macrobian Bow," "Fortunio," "The Story of Glaucus the Thessalian," and especially "The Wife of Brittany," all of which, he maintained, if published under Morris' name would "obtain at once a recognition on both sides of the Atlantic. We cannot see that the American poet is one whit inferior to his accomplished English contemporary in tenderness, sweetness, simplicity, grace, and ideal charm, while we venture to say that he has more than Morris, the true poetic enthusiasm, the unwithholding self-abandonment to the sentiment suggested by his themes." The critical charge of Morris' influence was not easily laid to rest, but Whipple's advocacy and Howells' retraction provided Hayne with some small satisfaction for an accusation which had rankled.

II *"Daphles"*

Hayne began to write "Daphles" in September, 1864, only a few weeks after he had completed "The Wife of Brittany"; but he did not get very far with it. He returned to it in 1868 and completed it a year later, as he wrote Mrs. Preston on September 6, 1869; "during the last 5 or 6 days I have composed the greater part of a story in verse, which finished late on Sat night, numbers some 600 lines in the heroic measure—not of Pope, but of Chaucer, & after him Keats, Hunt, and Morris! It is called simply, "Daphles," and the time & characters are Greek." He was pleased with the way the poem turned out; and, after it appeared in the *Southern Review* for January, 1870, he sent copies to Lowell, Whittier, Longfellow, Whipple, and Howells.

Subtitled "An Argive Story," "Daphles" occupies the place of honor in *Legends and Lyrics*; but it is assuredly not so good a poem as "The Wife of Brittany." Based on "The Fair Revenge" in Hunt's *Indicator* (Hayne's favorite "store-house of legendary lore"), which, in turn, is an amplification of an account first recorded in "Albion's England," "Daphles" is the story of a queen whose loyal subjects achieve a complete military victory over Doracles, a dissident vassal who considers himself as one with some right to the throne. Upon releasing the "insurgent chief" from captivity, Daphles falls in love with him; but, since he does not return her affection, she offers him her hand "in state and name alone." He accepts only to have the opportunity to seek the aid of other rebels, the queen's "bitterest foes." During his absence on the frontier, Daphles pines away and gradually loses her reason and finally her life. While still in possession of her faculties, she wills the throne to Doracles, who returns to accept it after her death. Now king, Doracles discovers a picture of Daphles which he takes to his "secret chamber" and which haunts him until, as "our old-world legend saith," he can bear it no longer and takes his life with "his own mad right arm" thrusting home the blade.

Although Hayne has once again turned to a favorite author and book for material, he has not improved on his source which, in itself, contains a basic weakness that also vitiates the poem—that is, both Hunt and Hayne overlay the Argive civilization with an atmosphere and a texture more common to the medieval period than to the ancient past. Though Doracles may not be a perfect knight, he is a feudal lord; and Daphles reminds one of other languishing medieval ladies whose love is not returned, and who live in accordance with the usual feudal practices. Indeed, the narrative may be viewed as a rather bookish nineteenth-century treatment of the medieval romance; it is not strange, therefore, that Hayne chose again the "heroic measure" of Chaucer for his legend.

"Daphles," however, has its virtues. There are passages that deserve to stand with the best that Hayne had written. A fair sample occurs early in the poem when the armies of Doracles and Daphles pass in review before the reader and the day of the bloody contest arrives:

> . . . one bluff October day,
> There rose a blare of trumpets far away,
> And sound of thronging hoofs which muffled came,
> Borne on the wind, like the dull noise of flame
> Half stifled in dense woodlands; then the wings
> Of the Queen's host, as each swift section flings
> The imperial banner proudly fluttering out,
> Spread from the royal centre. Hark! a shout,
> As from those thousand hearts in one great soul
> Sublimely fused, rose thunder-deep, to roll,
> In wild acclaim, far down the quivering van;
> And wilder still the heroic tumult ran
> From front to rear, when, through her palace gate,
> Daphles, in unaccustomed martial state,

A keen spear shimmering in its silver hold,
And on her brow the Argive crown of gold,
Flashed like a sunbeam on her warriors' sight.

. . . .

But soon the foeman's cohorts, like a sea,
With waves of steel, and foam of snow-white plumes,
Slowly emerged from out the forest glooms
In splendid pomp and antique pageantry.
An ominous pause! And then the trumpets high
Sounded the terrible onset, and the field
Rocked as with earthquake, and the thick air reeled
With clangors fierce from echoing hill to hill.

The description and the diction in the old-fashioned manner and movement, now swift, now stately, are calculated with shrewd effect to lead up to the "onset" itself, all achieved in well-managed Chaucerian couplets, which are themselves no mean achievement.

The story itself leaves something to be desired. Neither Daphles nor Doracles is conceived or developed as anything more than a particular stock type, and the relations between them are not generally to be accounted for by the canons of twentieth-century psychology, though the chief point made—the yearning for that which is not available—surely transcends the psychology of any mere period of time. But, as Lanier observed of "The Wife of Brittany," "the plot" (and characters, too, for that matter) "is only conceivable as a thing of the past" and "belongs to the curiosities of history." And, as I have already suggested, even the accoutrements of history—atmosphere and background—have been treated rather cavalierly in "Daphles."

The contemporary reaction to "Daphles" is worth noting. Whipple, Stoddard, and Mrs. Preston spoke well of it in reviews of *Legends and Lyrics*; and Whittier wrote Hayne on March 17, 1870, that the poem was "very admirably told" and that there were lines in it "which linger long in the ear, and find an echo in the head." [6] Edward Spencer, however, offered a more critical view in a letter to Hayne of March 13, 1872: "I am now better able to feel its profound moral and see how each part is attuned to the key of the chief motif. I still do not admire the character of Daphles, not because she is made to love an unworthy man, but because she loves too weakly and bends and is broken like the ineffective stem of the Nile lily. That, however, is a mere matter of taste. As she is shown, she contrasts most forcibly with Doracles."

A generation later in 1903 an even more favorable judgment of the poem was delivered by Ludwig Lewisohn in a series of articles on the history of literature in South Carolina for the Charleston *Sunday News*. His essay on Hayne's poetry is still one of the best critical treatments available. Though he preferred the nature poems, he thought the narratives "admirable": " 'Daphles,' 'The Wife of Brittany,' and 'The Story of Glaucus the Thessalian' are narrative poems of extraordinary beauty and power. The heroic couplet in which they are composed is managed with a skill akin to that of Keats and Morris. ... I know of no other American narrative poem that is at all comparable to 'Daphles.' "

This view is one with which few recent critics could agree, and Lewisohn himself later tempered it in *Expression in America* (1932). The revolution wrought by Robert Browning, E. A. Robinson, and Robert Frost, among others, makes Hayne's narrative poems seem old-fashioned and out-of-date—"Daphles" more so than "The Wife of Brittany" since Hunt's account offered Hayne less to work with than did Chaucer's tale. When related to like poems of the nineteenth century, Hayne's poems may be more aptly characterized for what they are—competent, finished pieces in the Romantic manner of Keats and Hunt and, to a degree, Morris, though it should be remembered that Hayne read *Earthly Paradise* after he had completed "The Wife of Brittany" and was well along on the composition of "Daphles." "Daphles" itself has not adequately stood the test of time. Its style is not in fashion and is not likely to be revived soon, but it possesses some small intrinsic merit and even more historical importance, for it is another manifestation of Hayne's affinity for the dominant Anglo-American poetic tradition of his day, a tradition under attack in his own generation by Whitman but since changed considerably by Emily Dickinson, W. B. Yeats, Ezra Pound, and T. S. Eliot.

III   *Shorter Narrative Poems*

"Cambyses and the Macrobian Bow" and "The Story of Glaucus the Thessalian" are, like the longer narratives, source poems. They are also "legends," but they are relatively brief and contain some variety in verse pattern and in structure. They seem, therefore, more effective as poetic entities, at least in regard to length, than "Daphles." Indeed, "Cambyses" is one of Hayne's best poems in this vein.

Based on the story as given in one of G. A. Lawrence's novels, though ultimately, of course, such material comes from Herodotus, "Cambyses" is a terse account in blank verse of a Persian ruler's cruel treatment of one of his subjects. When Prexaspes, one of Cambyses' courtiers, tells his comrades of a "certain Bactrian's matchless skill" with a bow, the King becomes envious and angry since he considers himself the "mightiest archer" in the realm. Prexaspes compounds his error, however, when he admits that not even Cambyses (especially a Cambyses who has tarried with the "beakers overlong") can hit a self-selected target. In response, Cambyses orders the young son of Prexaspes to serve as his mark and bends the "mammoth bow" until its "horns" almost meet. He shoots the arrow into the boy's heart and orders the bereft father to examine the child and testify to his marksmanship:

> . . . thus he went, and thus he saw
> What never in the noontide or the night,
> Awake or sleeping, idle or in toil,
> 'Neath the wild forest or the perfumed lamps
> Of palaces, shall leave his stricken sight
> Unblasted, or his spirit purged of woe.

Impotent and "white as death," the courtier can only make "meek obeisance to his King" and report that the child's heart has been "cloven, ye gods! in twain!" Cambyses, laughing until his beard quivers, "forgives" the man who had doubted his skill and commands him:

> Only when next these Persian dogs shall call
> Cambyses drunkard, rise, Prexaspes, rise!
> And tell them how, and to what purpose, once,
> Once, on a morn which followed hot and wan
> A night of monstrous revel and debauch,—
> Cambyses bent his huge Macrobian bow.

Stark and grim in a manner unlike much of his other poetry, Hayne set great store by this poem and could not understand

why some of the critics did not properly appreciate it. Particularly distressed by Howells' reaction to the piece, Hayne wrote Mrs.
Preston on December 23, 1873: "The 'ms' of 'The Macrobian
Bow' I offered to Howells. He was unaffectedly struck by what he
called its 'dramatic vigor,' but he nevertheless rejected it! And
why? Because, oh! ye Gods!—because the subject was *too painful*, & the 'strong picturesque treatment' only made it the more
agonizingly 'impressive'!!!" Furthermore, Howells suggested in
his review that "Cambyses" was too strong for his readers, for
Hayne caustically remarks to Mrs. Preston that the *Atlantic*'s
readers "must be as soft as pancakes, fit to 'die of a rose in aromatic pain.' " This strange rejection, coming as it does from the
future lord high priest of Realism, may reveal more about Howells' judgment of his readers' taste, or about his own editorial
crotchets, than about the merit of Hayne's poem.

Paradoxically, critics far more inclined toward the Romantic
than Howells liked "Cambyses." Mrs. Preston remarked on its
"tone and treatment" as that of an "ancient lyre with a quick
sharp twang"; Whipple considered it—along with "The Wife
of Brittany," "Daphles," and "The Story of Glaucus the Thessalian"—to be one of Hayne's best narratives; and Lanier, in a
letter of September 13, 1871, praised the poem in manuscript as
"vigorous and full of dramatic *verve*." " 'Tis a fearful tale," he
continued, "beautifully told. . . . The utter coolness of the cruelty
is brought out with great clearness; and the stroke of pain goes
to the heart of the reader, straight as Cambyses' arrow to the
heart of the page. The accessories, too . . . give a kind of heart-
lessness-of-atmosphere to the whole scene that frames it perfectly"
(*Works*, VIII, 175).

Whatever the contemporary critical verdict, "Cambyses and
the Macrobian Bow" remains after a century an excellent
poem of its type. It contains the usual flaws of much nineteenth-
century source poetry—the weak characters, the derivative nature of the materials, the poetic diction—but it creates, without
the mawkish sentimentality of which Hayne was sometimes capable and in an unaffected style different from his usual ornate
rhetoric, an unforgettable picture of power that begets per-
versity and that affects the lives of three human beings. These
people are not brought to life altogether or in the same manner.
Cambyses is a study in pride, whereas Prexaspes and his son

are sketched chiefly in terms of their painful predicament. The dramatic situation is based not on a contest of wills, for there is only one will that matters and that is the tyrant's. His cruelty knows no bounds; his pride brooks no challenge; and human nature means nothing to him. He is omnipotent and merciless, and opposition is impossible or meaningless. Accordingly, there is no hope for justice—no deity is concerned—and the tragic waste of human life suggests no resolution of a mighty issue but, instead, proves merely a means for a drunken despot to indulge his wounded vanity. Here indeed is a kind of ultimate example of man's inhumanity to his fellowman, and in this poem Hayne takes his place in the tradition of the great Romantics in condemning such cruelty and tyranny.

Like "Daphles" and "Avolio," "The Story of Glaucus the Thessalian" is based on Hunt's *Indicator* and puts Hayne in direct competition with Landor and Lowell, both of whom had already written poems about the same legend. Hunt's account of the hamadryad is based on Apollonius of Rhodes, and Hayne's verse is based on Hunt, though it is worth noting that the first version of the poem was called "The Hamadryad" in 1866 (Landor's piece had appeared under the same title in 1842), and two years later Hayne changed his title to "Rhoecus and the Dryad" (Lowell's "Rhoecus" had come out in 1844).

Following Hunt rather closely, Hayne tells the "story" of a selfish young Thessalian who, in a moment of "genial sympathy," saves a tree from falling and is rewarded by the nymph of the tree with a wish to be fulfilled. Glaucus, taken by "her maiden sweetness deified," asks for her hand. The request is granted, but later in the day when the nymph's messenger, a "swift, shining, yellow-breasted bee," sounds its "small alarum" to bring Glaucus to the trysting place, the selfish youth is too busy at dice to consider leaving until he has won the stakes. Too late, he rushes off to seek his new love; no longer can he see her:

> . . . nevermore on thee
> Shall visions of that finer world above
> Dawn from the chaste auroras of their love;
> But common things, seen in a funeral haze
> Of earthiness, and sorrow, and mistrust,
> Weigh the soul down, and soil its hopes with dust. . . .

He has lost the hope of looking into nature's "innermost heart"
and of sharing the "bliss" of spiritual "Immortality" with the nymph.
Bereft and dismayed, Glaucus discovers that he is once more
"alone."

The legend is recounted with a minimum of effort and flourish,
and the couplets are varied occasionally by triplets and delayed
rhyme. Though nature is celebrated, the diction is conventionally
poetic and hardly that of the language of men. The theme is obvious, and the poet's intention is clear; but no moral is obtruded
on the reader. A poem of some slight charm, Howells' characterization of it as "a delicate and tenderly sympathetic version" of the
legend is fair enough; but the poem lacks the power and impact
of "Cambyses and the Macrobian Bow" and seems less conse-
quential when compared directly with it. Yet, as Jay B. Hubbell
has indicated, "The Story of Glaucus the Thessalian" holds its
own with the pieces on the same legend by Landor and Lowell.[7]

IV *The Lyrics*

Hayne's lyrics appealed to some of the critics more than his
legends, and a number of them deserve consideration here. Among
these are his elegy to the memory of Timrod; the pieces addressed
to his wife, mother, and son; the introspective poems about his
own situation; several sonnets; and such miscellaneous items as
"A Summer Mood," "The River," and "Fire Pictures."

"Under the Pine. To the Memory of Henry Timrod" "came
from the very depths of my heart," Hayne wrote Edward Spencer
on March 20, 1872; but, he added, "on that very account I tried
to maintain a reserve of feeling and passion."[8] This reserve is
noticeable in the poem, for it is in the elegiac tradition of "Lycidas,"
"Adonais," and "Thyrsis," though it is hardly in the pastoral form.
Nature is not absent (indeed, the pine in question was located,
according to Hayne, in a "superb pine forest just opposite . . .
'Copse Hill' "); but it is a formal nature closer to Arnold perhaps
than to Wordsworth.

In the beginning a "majestic Pine" reminds the poet of his loss
and prompts him to reflect yearningly about it:

> The same majestic Pine is lifted high
> > Against the twilight sky,
> The same low, melancholy music grieves
> > Amid the topmost leaves,
> As when I watched, and mused, and dreamt with him,
> > Beneath these shadows dim.
>
> O Tree! hast thou no memory at thy core
> > Of one who comes no more?

The speaker, who continues to address the tree, wonders if his friend's "poet-touch" and dreams have not "stirred" its "nature dark"; for everything about the "forest-king"—leaves, boughs, vines, cones—"speaks" of the departed, and especially "between the twilight and the night" does he feel his comrade "near":

> Still as the grave which holds his tranquil form,
> > Hushed after many a storm,—
> Still as the calm that crowns his marble brow,
> > No pain can wrinkle now,—
> Still as the peace—pathetic peace of God—
> > That wraps the holy sod,
>
> Where every flower from our dead minstrel's dust
> > Should bloom, a type of trust,—
> That faith which waxed to wings of heavenward might
> > To bear his soul from night,—
> That faith, dear Christ! whereby we pray to meet
> > His spirit at God's feet!

True feeling is held under control and expressed in competent verse, but the development of the thought is not adequate to the lament for the dead minstrel. In this poem Hayne seems to be on the verge of saying something memorable, yet he brings the elegy to a climax with the mixed imagery and awkward structure of the last stanza.

Some critics thought well of "Under the Pine." Whipple, in the *Evening Transcript*, listed it with several other pieces illustrating Hayne's "mastery of various forms of poetic expression," and Stoddard chose the "manly, heartfelt dirge in memory of Timrod" and two or three other poems as his preferences among the lyrics in his review for the *Aldine*. It is interesting to note, however, that neither Mrs. Preston nor Lanier mentioned this elegy in their respective notices of *Legends and Lyrics.*

Hayne's lyrics to various members of his family are among the best of his short poems in this collection. Several of these deal with his wife, the most important of which, aside from the dedication, are "From the Woods," "An Anniversary," and "The Bonny Brown Hand." In the first of these the speaker, Hayne himself, characterizes the outrageous fortune which has beset him; but he concludes that all is not lost, for "thou still art here, soul of my soul, my Wife!" "An Anniversary" celebrates both his marriage to Minna Hayne and the event itself in retrospect.

Of the pieces addressed to his wife, Hayne most cherished "The Bonny Brown Hand." Published first in *Appletons' Journal* for November 20, 1869, the poem was an immediate favorite with Hayne's readers; for, despite one or two elements of fantasy (the references to "our children's voices" and to a "nestling" daughter could hardly apply to the Hayne family), the sincerity of the sentiment of some of the lines goes to the heart:

> Let me feel your glowing fingers
> In a clasp that warms and lingers
> With the full, fond love of earth,
> Till the joy of love's completeness
> In this flush of fireside sweetness,
> Shall brim our hearts with spirit-wine, outpoured beside the hearth.
> So steal your little hand in mine, while twilight falters down,—
> That little hand, that fervent hand, that hand of bonny brown,—
> The hand which points the path to heaven, yet makes a
> heaven of earth.

The romantic sentiment of this lyric may not make up for its lack of esthetic distance, but it appealed to many readers in the nineteenth century. A writer in the London *Literary World* for January 9, 1874, thought nothing in the entire volume "more tender, healthful and true" than "The Bonny Brown Hand"; and Edward Spencer wrote Hayne on March 13, 1872: "*The Bonny Brown Hand,* in metre, in feeling, in quaint tenderness of touch, and shy frankness of heart-opening, is my favorite of all the book. The form is well nigh perfect, and the poem reminds me continually of Browning's delicious song in 'A Blot on the 'Scutcheon.'"

"Will" is an openhearted and unabashed revelation of Hayne's love for his son, his *"second self,"* published first in *Appletons' Journal* for January 13, 1872. Recalling in the first stanza the dread Hayne felt when the boy contracted a "child-illness of the brain," the poet is grateful in the second that Will survived:

> But Heaven was kind, Death passed you by;
> And now upon your arm I lean,
> *My second self,* of clearer eye,
> Of firmer nerve, and sturdier mien;
> Through you, methinks, my long-lost youth
> Revives, from whose sweet founts of truth,
> And joy, I drink my fill:
> I feel your every heart-throb, know
> What inmost hopes within you glow,—
> One soul's between us, Will!

Finally, the poet prays that "this be always so" and that, while his life "endures,"

> It aye may sympathize with yours
> In thought, aim, action still;
> That you, O son (till comes the end),
> In me may find your comrade, friend,
> And *more* than father, Will!

This honest emotion is expressed in diction which is neither cloying nor extravagant but, with the exception of one or two flourishes, appropriate. As Stoddard observed in the *Aldine,* " 'Will' is a valuable addition to the *personal* poetry of the time."

In "To My Mother," however, Hayne becomes consciously poetic in considering his debt to his parent, in choosing diction more pertinent to his mother's day than to his own, and in remembering that this lyric will close the volume:

> I bless thee, Dear, with reverent thought!
> Pale face, and tresses hoary,
> Whose every silvery thread hath caught
> Some hint of heavenly glory;—
> To thee, with trust assured, sublime,
> Death's angel-call that waitest,—
> To thee, as once my earliest rhyme,
> Lo! now, I bring—my latest!

Still, his wife and family are his chief sources of strength. His most meaningful contribution on this theme is the aforementioned "From the Woods" (*Lippincott's,* May 1868), a piece which sums up well his views on the compensations of his "lot." He realizes of course that his position is not altogether advantageous, yet nature sustains him with its "solemn pine-groves" and "multitudinous sylvan choir," and "rare books"—Shakespeare's consoling "philosophies" and Milton's "deep thunder"—offer "spiritual" nourishment; but, "more than all," he concludes, his "nobler life shines on unquenched" in the "deathless love" of the "soul" of his soul, his wife.

The sonnets cover the same general range of themes touched upon in the other lyrics—poets, nature, Hayne's personal situation, the passage of time, and death. In separate sonnets devoted to William Morris and Leigh Hunt, Hayne pays his respects to two of his English contemporaries whose work meant much to him. The first he sees as Chaucer's successor ("alone on thee/ Fall the rich bays which bloomed round Chaucer's head!"), and the second as the "clearest, cleanest nature given to man/ In these, our latter days." "Poets" (*Galaxy,* March 15, 1867) takes up a theme announced earlier in "Great Poets and Small" and sounds the same note of self-justification: there is a place on "bright Parnassus" for all orders of poets, from those "master minstrels" who "thunder on the heights" to those near the base who "chant lowlier measures."

A beneficent nature comes in for its share of attention, one that, to be sure, is generally indigenous to the South but that is celebrated in diction more characteristic of the eighteenth-century British tradition than of nineteenth-century Romantic vocabulary. "Sylvan Musings. In May," for example, offers the meditations of a speaker who, tranquilized by the sights and sounds of May, describes his locale in stylized poetic language and complacently contemplates bees and birds without insecticide or adequate cover and never even suggests that chiggers and mosquitoes may lurk in the vicinity:

> Couched in cool shadow, girt by billowy swells
> Of foliage, rippling into buds and flowers,
> Here I repose o'erfanned by breezy bowers,—
> Lulled by a delicate stream whose music wells
> Tender and low through those luxuriant dells,

Wherefrom a single broad-leaved chestnut towers;—
Still musing in the long, lush, languid hours,—
As in a dream I heard the tinkling bells
Of far-off kine, glimpsed through the verdurous sheen,
Blent with faint bleatings from the distant croft,—
The bee-throngs murmurous in the golden fern,
The wood-doves veiled by depths of flickering green,—
And near me, where the wild "queen fairies" burn,
The thrush's bridal passion, warm and soft!

In another, called merely "Sonnet," Hayne begins to discover more specifically his "local habitation"; for, though the method and diction are still traditional, the jasmine and mockingbird obviously belong to his own surroundings at Copse Hill:

Of all the woodland flowers of earlier spring,
These golden jasmines, each an air-hung bower,
Meet for the Queen of Fairies' tiring hour,
Seem loveliest and most fair in blossoming;—
How yonder mock-bird thrills his fervid wing
And long, lithe throat, where twinkling flower on flower
Rains the globed dewdrops down, a diamond shower,
O'er his brown head, poised as in act to sing;—
Lo! the swift sunshine floods the flowery urns,
Girding their delicate gold with matchless light,
Till the blent life of bough, leaf, blossom, burns;
Then, then outbursts the mock-bird clear and loud,
Half-drunk with perfume, veiled by radiance bright,—
A star of music in a fiery cloud!

This slight movement away from a rather bookish treatment of nature is of a piece with Hayne's general effort during the early 1870's to examine his own area more closely and to express in his poems a somewhat Wordsworthian attitude toward nature.

Nevertheless, the sonnets on his personal situation are seldom couched in the common language of men. "The Cottage on the Hill," for example, though obviously a sketch of the "homestead" at Copse Hill, is described in such "sylvan" surroundings, among "rills," "wood-fays," "moist bay-leaves," and "clouds fantastical" that it is difficult to remember that the humble house in question was "rudely built of unseasoned lumber and clap-boards of pine." When Hayne considered the plight of his mother state, however, he was inspired to write in "Carolina" a melancholy *cri de coeur* which, despite its poetic devices and conventional diction, remains a moving lyric:

> That fair young land which gave me birth is dead!
> Lost as a fallen star that quivering dies
> Down the pale pathway of Autumnal skies,
> A vague faint radiance flickering where it fled;
> All she hath wrought, all she hath planned or said,
> Her golden eloquence, her high emprise,
> Wrecked, on the languid shore of Lethe lies,
> While cold Oblivion veils her piteous head:
> O mother! loved and loveliest! debonair
> As some brave Queen of antique chivalries,—
> Thy beauty's blasted like thy desolate coasts;—
> Where now thy lustrous form, thy shining hair?
> Where thy bright presence, thine imperial eyes?
> Lost in dim shadows of the realm of Ghosts!

As Hayne lamented the difference between Carolina's past and present, so the passage of time led him in another "Sonnet" to offer a view of death characteristic of this period of his life:

> I fear thee not, O Death! nay, oft I pine
> To clasp thy passionless bosom to mine own,—
> And on thy heart sob out my latest moan,
> Ere lapped and lost in thy strange sleep divine;
> But much I fear lest that chill breath of thine
> Should freeze all tender memories into stone,—
> Lest ruthless and malign Oblivion
> Quench the last spark that lingers on love's shrine:—
> O God! to moulder through dark, dateless years,—
> The while all loving ministries shall cease,
> And Time assuage the fondest mourner's tears!—
> Here lies the sting!—this, *this* it is to die!—
> And yet great Nature rounds all strife with peace,
> And life or death,—each rests in mystery!

Compounded of elements of Hamlet's soliloquy, Tennyson's *In Memoriam,* Wordsworth's nature, and his own "drear forgetfulness," this poem suggests something of the derivative nature of Hayne's poetic thought at this stage of his literary career.

Altogether, these sonnets are among the best he had written. Edward Spencer and Maurice Thompson praised several of them, and Mrs. Preston considered them "as perfect . . . as [any] our country has produced." They may, she points out in the *Southern Magazine* (1872), readily stand comparison with Rossetti's or Wordsworth's sonnets in theme or construction. Wordsworth, she concludes, "gives us Etruscan vases," whereas Hayne "carves his cup somewhat after the Cellini fashion." This is high praise, and surely the partial judgment of a friend, but as Hubbell has observed in *The South in American Literature:* Hayne's "best work, early or late, appears in his sonnets. . . . After his friends Longfellow and George Henry Boker, he was perhaps the best American sonneteer of his time" (747).

Of the remaining lyrics in the volume, three deserve attention: "A Summer Mood," "The River," and "Fire Pictures." The first of these, written in 1870, was enclosed in a letter of July 21 to Oliver Wendell Holmes; for, though the epigraph is from one of Thomas Heywood's plays, Hayne wrote Holmes that the "ground-thought" was suggested by a passage in *The Autocrat of the Breakfast Table.* "Who has not," he queried his friend, "sometimes experienced a sort of inward spiritual convulsion at the discord which seems to prevail between the mystic soul of Nature, and the soul of Man? Such is the conception I have tried to embody in 'A Summer Mood' ":

> Ah! me, for evermore, for evermore
> These human hearts of ours must yearn and sigh,
> While down the dells and up the murmurous shore
> Nature renews her immortality.

The "heavens of June" are calm and June roses are beautiful, but human beings "mourn in a world which breathes of Paradise." The sunshine "mocks the tears it may not dry," and the breezes "blow their gay trumpets in the face of care" whereas the "bolder winds" "rack" the "humbled souls" of men:

> The field-birds seem to twit us as they pass
> With their small blisses, piped so clear and loud;
> The cricket triumphs o'er us in the grass,
> And the lark, glancing beamlike up the cloud,

Sings us to scorn with his keen rhapsodies:
      Small things and great unconscious tauntings bring
To edge our cares, whilst we, the proud and wise,
      Envy the insect's joy, the birdling's wing!

And thus for evermore, till time shall cease,
      Man's soul and Nature's—each a separate sphere—
Revolves, the one in discord, one in peace,
      And who shall make the solemn mystery clear?

Both Howells and Lanier viewed this lyric as one manifesting, to use Howells' phrase, "flavors of the Southern air and soil"; and Lanier cited the stanza about the field birds as a "genuine snatch caught from out the sedges of a Southern field." Each considered the poem one of the best in the book, Howells quoting it completely in his review in the *Atlantic* (1872), and Lanier characterizing it, along with the dedicatory piece, in the *Southern Magazine* (1875), as the "nearest approach to the ideal of lyric poetry" in the collection.

Neither Howells nor Lanier mentioned "The River" (*Appletons' Journal,* October 1, 1870), though in idea and movement at least this lyric anticipates Lanier's "Song of the Chattahoochee" (1877) without obtruding a moral on its basic analogy, which relates the movement of the water from source to sea to seasons in the life of man. Thus man's life, like the river, runs its course from "dew-lit fallows" and "golden shallows" to the tides of a "strong, swift, glorious" stream rolling and rushing onward until the "cloud-racks" gather, the "ominous thunder" knolls, the storm breaks, and a "blissful calm" follows:

Thence again with quaintest ranges,
      On the fateful streamlet rolled
Through unnumbered, nameless changes,
      Shade and sunshine, gloom and gold,
Till the tides, grown sad and weary,
      Longed to meet the mightier main,
And their low-toned *miserere*
      Mingled with his grand refrain;
Oh, the languid, lapsing river,
      Weak of pulse and soft of tune,—
Lo! the *sun* hath set forever,
      Lo! the ghostly moon!

But thenceforth through moon and starlight
    Sudden-swift the streamlet's sweep;
Yearning for the mystic far-light,
    Pining for the solemn deep;
While the old strength gathers o'er it,
    While the old voice rings sublime,
And in pallid mist before it,
    Fade the phantom shows of time,—
Till with one last eddying quiver,
    All its checkered journey done,
Seaward breaks the ransomed river,
    Goal and grave are won!

The last two stanzas Spencer thought "very perfect," both in the echoing flow of their rhythm and in the solemn pattern of their sentiment. He did not hesitate to point out (quite rightly) in his letter of March 13, 1872, a "somewhat confused" treatment of geography but only because, he observed, "this poem is so fine, so full of deep, solemn, serene melody that I want to see it faultless in point of landscape." There is indeed "melody," and also movement: but, for some reason, these seem to militate against the diction (Hayne is as fond of compound words as Lanier is later) and the logical thought of the poem. Less didactic and onomatopoetic than Lanier's "Song of the Chattahoochee," Hayne's "The River" is in these ways, despite its obvious faults and lack of prominence, possibly more acceptable to modern critical tastes than the better-known poem.

A lyric in the Poe manner, "Fire Pictures," is a tour de force which Lanier thought "in point of variety and delicacy of fancy . . . quite the best in the collection" and "in point of pure music" worthy of being placed beside "Edgar Poe's *Bells*," an experiment in onomatopoeia which it parallels in idea and movement if not in actual rhythm or meter.[9] The first sections of the two poems suggest the relationship:

"Fire Pictures"
O! the rolling, rushing Fire!
  O! the Fire!
How it rages, wilder, higher,
Like a hot heart's fierce desire,
Thrilled with passion that
  appalls us,
Half appalls, and yet enthralls us,
  O! the madly mounting Fire!

Up it sweepeth,—wave and
  quiver,—
Roaring like an angry river,—
  O! the Fire!—
Which an earthquake backward
  turneth,
Backward o'er its riven courses,
Backward to its mountain sources,
While the blood-red sunset
  burneth,
Like a God's face grand
  with ire,—
  O! the bursting, billowy Fire!

"The Bells"
*The bells!—*hear the bells!
The *merry* wedding bells!
The *little* silver bells!
How fairy-like a melody *there*
  swells
From the silver tinkling bells
Of the bells, bells, bells!
  Of the bells!

The bells!—ah, the bells!
The heavy iron bells!
Hear the tolling of the bells!
  Hear the knells!
How horrible a monody *there* floats
  From their throats—
  From their deep-toned throats!
How I shudder at the notes
  From the melancholy throats
Of the bells, bells, bells—
  Of the bells—[10]

"Fire Pictures," too long to quote in its entirety, is, in brief, a series of "pictures" suggested, as Hayne wrote Mrs. Preston on December 15, 1871, by the "gorgeous flames of blessed 'pine-knots.'" Moving swiftly from "flickering" to "roaring," the fire excites visions of "Vesuvian lavas," the destruction of "prairie seas" and of "martyr-saints," the "interior" of a Dutch tavern with its "Toper," and transports the "I" of the poem on a dreamlike odyssey to a "happy plain/ Sloping towards the Southern main" where exists a sort of lotos-land atmosphere and from there to a "nether Universe" of "Titan spires" and "Cyclopean halls" where the visions falter as the fire sinks to embers.

Several of these passages represent adequately the poem's various qualities. The Dutch "interior," for example, suggests a seventeenth-century genre painting though the treatment of scene and character is closer to that of Washington Irving than of Jan Vermeer. Within a tavern

Sits a Toper, stout and yellow,
Blinking o'er his steamy bowl;
    Hugely drinking,
    Slyly winking,
As the pot-house Hebé passes,
With a clink and clang of glasses;
Ha! 'tis plain, the stout old fellow—
As his wont is—waxes mellow,
Nodding 'twixt each dreamy leer,
Swaying in his elbow chair,
Next to one,—a portly Peasant,—
Pipe in hand, whose swelling cheek,
Jolly, rubicund, and sleek,
Puffs above the blazing coal;
While his heavy, half-shut eyes
Watch the smoke wreaths evanescent,
Eddying lightly as they rise,
Eddying lightly and aloof
Toward the great, black, oaken roof!

Even better, to Lanier at least, is the lotos-land strophe:

    Ah! the Fire!
    Gently glowing,
    Fairly flowing,
Like a rivulet rippling deep
Through the meadow-lands of sleep,
Bordered where its music swells,
By the languid lotos-bells,
And the twilight asphodels;
Mingled with a richer boon
Of queen-lilies, each a moon,
Orbèd into white completeness;
O! the perfume! the rare sweetness
Of those grouped and fairy flowers,
Over which the love-lorn hours
Linger,—not alone for them,
Though the lotos swings its stem
With a lulling stir of leaves,—
Though the lady-lily laves
Coy feet in the crystal waves,
And silvery undertune
From some mystic wind-song grieves

> Dainty-sweet, amid the bells
> Of the twilight asphodels;
> But because a charm more rare
> Glorifies the mellow air,
> In the gleam of lifted eyes,
> In the tranquil ecstasies
> Of two lovers, leaf-embowered,
>   Lingering there,—
> Each of whose fair lives hath flowered,
> Like the lily-petals finely,
> Like the asphodel divinely.

This passage, Lanier on March 20, 1871, wrote Hayne is the "glory and fair climax of the poem, the sweetest notes, to my mind, and the fullest of genuine poet's music, that you have ever sung." Furthermore, he continued: "Nothing you have ever done has pleased me so entirely: and I believe the verdict of after-poets will support me."

Despite this praise for the climax, Lanier later manages in his review to give its due to the last strophe, where "at one and the same time, by the devices of onomatopeia [sic] and of rhythmical imitation, are doubly interpreted the sob of a man and the flicker of a flame so perfectly that sob, flicker, word, rhythm, each appears to represent the other, and to be used convertibly with the other in such will-o'-the-wisp transfigurations as quite vanish in mere description":

> Ah, the faint and flickering Fire!
>   Ah, the Fire!
> Like a young man's transient ire,
> Like an old man's last desire,
> Lo! it falters, dies!
>   Still, I see,
>   But brokenly, but mistily,
>   Fall and rise,
>   Rise and fall,
>   Ghosts of shifting phantasy;
> Now the embers, smouldered all,
> Sink to ruin; sadder dreams
> Follow on their vanished gleams;
> Wailingly the spirits call,
> Spirits on the night-winds solemn,
> Wraiths of happy Hopes that left me. . . .

The foregoing remarks clearly suggest that "Fire Pictures" should be read aloud, and Lanier makes the point explicitly in the *Southern Magazine* (1875); the poem is, he asserts, "true recitativo." "The energy of its movements, the melody of its metres, the changes of its rhythm, the variety of its fancies, the artistic advance to its climax, particularly the management of its close, . . . all these elements," he maintains, "require for full enjoyment that the actual music of the poem should fall upon the ear."

Such poetry, of course, contains within its very nature and purpose certain qualities, usually sing-song meter and forced or affected diction, which militate against its perfection. In his review, Lanier comments on "two classes" of "faults" in "Fire Pictures" and, indeed, in all Hayne's poetry—faults which, ironically, might also apply to Lanier's poetry. The first he characterizes as a "frequently-recurring *lapsus* of thought" in which the poet "falls into trite similes, worn collocations of words, and commonplace sentiments"; the second is "diffuseness, principally originating in a lavishness and looseness of adjectives." No reader has to look far in "Fire Pictures" to find these flaws and others. Despite them and the dated quality of the style, this poem deserves consideration as an indication of one aspect of Hayne's technique and as a manifestation of Poe's influence on his younger contemporaries. Moreover, as Hubbell suggests in *The South in American Literature,* "Fire Pictures" may serve as a fair example of Lanier's indebtedness to Hayne's poetry (777).

Hayne was not unaware of the faults of "Fire Pictures" and of his poems in general. On January 24, 1872, he wrote Mrs. Preston about his standards for *Legends and Lyrics:* "Nothing . . . which does not possess—in the words of my dear, dead friend Henry Timrod—some 'body of Thought,' or, some expression of feeling, or fancy, not altogether *ephemeral,* but belonging to the *permanent* in emotion, if not in Art! Such was the ideal aimed at! Of course, *of course I* missed the mark, but I shall be satisfied if the 'miss' was not absolute, awkward, complete!"

This view verges on false modesty, for *Legends and Lyrics* was an "advance" on Hayne's earlier work and he knew it. So did the critics. Whipple, Thompson, and Mrs. Preston pointed this out.[11] Bayard Taylor wrote Hayne on March 25, 1872: "I think this much the best volume you have published. The poems show a finer finish, a greater symmetry, both of form and idea, than your earlier ones. I am very glad to see this, because it confirms my impression that you recognize the true nature of the poetic art, which, indeed, is that of all art—proportion. . . . It was evident in your former volumes, but they show less patient elaboration than this last." [12] In a review in the Indianapolis *Journal* for November 14, 1874, Maurice Thompson, with Hayne's "Poets" in mind, concluded: "He is not precisely a lyric poet, nor is he quite one of the thunderers on the heights of song. He seems to me very nearly the golden mean between De Beranger and Milton, a scholarly, graceful singer, dreamful rather than imaginative, as truly Southern as a palmetto tree. . . . I know of no truer poet than Hayne." Hayne did not have to be told that he had arrived as a poet. All he had to do was develop what had been acknowledged by his peers.

CHAPTER 4

The Mountain of the Lovers, 1875

L ESS than two years after the appearance of *Legends and Lyrics* in 1872, Hayne had another volume of poems ready for the press. He could not, however, find a publisher willing to bring it out on terms suitable to him. By April, 1874, Osgood, Hurd and Houghton, and Roberts and Brothers in Boston; E. J. Hale in New York; and Lippincott in Philadelphia had all "refused" his new collection. "All of them," he wrote Mrs. Preston the following October, "I have yet tried, willingly undertake *half the expenses* of the work, and offer a fair percentage on sales; but I had hoped they would take *all* the risks at this late day (the 11th hour of my artistic existence!)." On December 1, he noted bitterly that his latest manuscript had been "rejected by *every prominent belles lettres Publishing House* in the U. States!" Yet, he added sarcastically, "they accept the performances of the Nora Perrys, the Miss Hudsons, the whole 'mob of gentlewomen & gentlemen' that 'write with ease,' (but furnish heavy reading), as if they were of the 'few, the immortal names that were not born to die!' "

Finally, early in 1875, E. J. Hale and Son, the New York firm which had published Hayne's edition of Timrod's poems, examined the manuscript a second time and agreed to publish it on the basis of an "advance" from Hayne with the understanding between them that this sum should be returned to the poet from the sale of the book and that sales thereafter should be shared on the usual basis. Under these terms the first unbound copies of *The Mountain of the Lovers; With Poems of Nature and Tradition* were mailed in May, 1875; and the book itself appeared in June.

The Mountain of the Lovers is, with the exception of the title piece and one or two others, a collection of Hayne's verse published in periodicals between 1872 and 1875. Not unlike *Legends and*

Lyrics in content, it offers, for example, several narratives
("legends" are called "poems of tradition"), a number of lyrics
(many of which deal with nature), another elegy on Timrod, a
few personal poems, and some sonnets. It differs from the preceding volume chiefly in its stress on nature in the shorter pieces and
in the frequency of their appearance and in the lack of such a
tour de force as "Fire Pictures." Whatever advance may be observed between the two collections is primarily the result of this
heightened awareness of and response to the natural world of
Copse Hill and Columbia County, Georgia.

This note was sounded in the very beginning in the dedication
to Mrs. Preston, a friend through correspondence for almost a decade yet one whom Hayne had never met and was destined never
to see. "Deathless sympathy," he exclaimed, bound their "hearts
and minds" even though the lady sang on the "mountain side" and
he "below" on the "plain." Surrounded by "joyous sylvan things"
amid the "flash of wings, / The rivulet's lapse, the breeze's play,"
the poet of the plain offers his gift of "wild-wood lays."

The nature theme, however, is suspended; and the collection
begins with the title poem and still another narrative—a revised
version of "Avolio" now called "The Vengeance of the Goddess
Diana"—to which are added later in the volume two narratives of
a slightly different character: "Frida and Her Poet" and "The Visit
of Mahmoud Ben Suleim to Paradise." The nature theme is resumed
after "The Vengeance of the Goddess Diana" in a series of lyrics
beginning with "The Voice in the Pines" and continuing from time
to time throughout the rest of the work, even in some pieces on
other topics, such as "By the Grave of Henry Timrod" and certain
personal poems and sonnets. Of course, some of these poems also
deal with other subjects. Finally, there is "Lucifer's Deputy," one
of Hayne's infrequent efforts at humor. The collection as a whole
leaves the impression that it is not so rich in scope and variety as
Legends and Lyrics.

I *"The Mountain of the Lovers"*

The most ambitious poem in the volume is the title piece itself,
a narrative composed in a modification of the ottava rima stanza
(*ababbacc* rather than *ababababcc*) and one too long for periodical
publication (Henry Mills Alden of *Harper's Monthly* declined it

for that reason in March, 1874). In a traditional form similar to
that of "Avolio," "Daphles," and "Glaucus the Thessalian," "The
Mountain of the Lovers" is like its predecessors in that it is also
based on one of Leigh Hunt's works, in this instance "The Mountain of the Two Lovers" in *The Companion.*

Hayne has taken some liberties with his source, but the romantic
story about the complications wrought by a highborn lady's love
for a serf despite her stern father's disapproval remains basically
the same. The chief difference between source and poem is that the
American poet seeks to give reasonable motivation to the three
chief characters and to introduce an element of mystery at the end.
Moreover, in a prefatory note, Hayne, though he justifies the privi-
lege of the poetic imagination to "elevate" a hill into a mountain,
seeks to explain such a phenomenon logically and to account rea-
sonably for certain extravagant details in his source.

The theme of the poem is stated in the first stanza:

> Love scorns degrees! the low he lifteth high,
> The high he draweth down to that fair plain
> Whereon, in his divine equality,
> Two loving hearts may meet, nor meet in vain;
> 'Gainst such sweet levelling Custom cries amain,
> But o'er its harshest utterance one bland sigh,
> Breathed passion-wise, doth mount victorious still,
> For Love, earth's lord, must have his lordly will.

Love has its will in the passion of Catrine, the beautiful daughter
of Earl Godolf, and Oswald, a handsome but lowborn serf. When
Godolf, a harsh and cruel baron whose demesne is in the Welsh
marches, discovers that his daughter loves a forester, he decrees
that Oswald must "bear aloft" the "blameful maid" to the mountain
top; if he "gain the height, untamed, unthrown," he may take
Catrine away "unharmed." The test established, Oswald takes up
his winsome burden and "moves in measured wise to dare his fate"
against the rugged slopes and rocky precipice. Despite these terrible obstacles and a final obstruction—"a savage cliff of beetling
brow"—Oswald carries Catrine to the summit, where, "linked in
close embrace," the two "fall headlong down," supine and "move-
less on the conquered hill." Godolf and his serfs rush to the top, the
Earl accusing Oswald of being in league with "the fiend" and de-

manding that the lovers be parted. But it is too late. Death has united them at last.

At this point Hunt ends his account, but Hayne is not so wise. In a sort of epilogue, he continues the action with a Poesque scene in which, during a "wild night" following the trial, Godolf at "wassail" bans his dead daughter. At that moment in the "red dusk" a "vague Shape," unperceived by the revelers, steals into the poem, reaches the "banquet board" with "raised sword," and kills the "caitiff lord." No sooner has the awful Shape acted than it departs; and, when one "death-pale reveler" cries aloud to the others to join him in flight, they follow him precipitately:

> In haste, in horror, and great tumult, fled
> The affrighted guests; then on the vacant room
> No maddening voice thenceforth disquieted,
> Fell the stern presence of a ghastly gloom.
> A place 'twas deemed of hopeless, baleful doom;
> Barred from all mortal view in darkness dread,
> Only the spectral forms of woe and sin
> Thro' the long years cold harborage found therein.

The critics had little to say about "The Mountain of the Lovers," although several thought well of it. Whipple in the Boston *Evening Transcript* for June 22, 1875, classed it with "The Vengeance of the Goddess Diana" and "Frida and Her Poet" and characterized all three as "melodious, and combining the interest of a connected story with the charm which springs from flowing ease of musical diction, brilliant fancy and suggestive thought." A reviewer in the *Aldine* pronounced the poem "charmingly told."

On the other hand, a writer in *Appletons' Journal* for June 26, 1875, noted the limitations of the narrative poems in the collection. He admitted that they were "musical and graceful," but he also considered them lacking in "vigor" and in the attainment of that "localization in time and space which is so essential in the treatment of these old tales." Maurice Thompson forthrightly remarked in the Indianapolis *Journal* for May 29, 1875, that Hayne "fails" when "he attempts strong dramatic effects, and he does himself infinite injustice when he forces his energies in their direction." Hayne himself later acknowledged privately that he had erred in publishing the piece. He admitted his mistake to John G. James on November 14, 1877; and he wrote Charles Warren Stoddard on December 24:

"The chief narrative was composed in a very unlucky vein, and I bitterly regret its publication."[1]

Thompson and Hayne are both right about "The Mountain of the Lovers." Hayne's forte was neither drama nor narrative; indeed, like Poe and Lanier and others whose genius was primarily lyrical, Hayne found it difficult to write a successful long poem, though "The Wife of Brittany" may be considered a general exception to this view and "Avolio" and "Daphles" partial ones.

"The Mountain of the Lovers" is derivative in theme and material. The treatment is conventional, and the narrative never really gets off the ground. The ottava rima stanza is quite adequate for the purposes of narrative, as Ariosto, Tasso, Byron, and others have shown; yet Hayne's modification of it tends to slow down the movement rather than to convey it. Though some motivation is established, the characters are types in the age-old situation of young lovers of different backgrounds forced to challenge a disapproving parent. The one feature Hayne seeks to add—the element of mystery at the end—seems, on the one hand, rather superfluous in terms of the story itself (especially as Hunt has given it) and, on the other, obtrusively didactic—a nice irony since the idea of the ending (without the didactic overtones) and even some of the diction are strongly Poesque.

Altogether, the poem fails to show any advance in technique or in the handling of the genre, one which had attracted the poet and challenged him for over twenty years. It is no wonder, then, that Hayne later thought he had made a "grave mistake" in placing "The Mountain of the Lovers" "at the head of the vol [sic]" (*Letters*, 418). In a psychological sense, as well as a critical one, the poem failed to impress Hayne's audience as a sign of progress in his literary development.

II *"The Vengeance of the Goddess Diana"*

This narrative had appeared first as "Avolio; A Legend of the Island of Cos" in *Russell's Magazine* and had been reprinted later as the title poem in Hayne's third collection of verse (see Chapter 2). Remembering the critical charges regarding Morris' influence on "The Wife of Brittany" and other long poems, Hayne added a prefatory note to "The Vengeance of the Goddess Diana" in which he described the publishing history and revision of the piece and asserted a "humble claim of precedence in the poetical treatment of *this* legend."

The new version offers a number of brief changes in lines here and there, some new paragraph breaks, and two important expansions of passages. The first of these seeks to explain Avolio's response to the serpent on religious grounds as well as on those of fear and revulsion. The second develops further in the context of the serpent's situation two ideas which had long fascinated Hayne: the relationships between man and nature and between the good and the beautiful. His treatment of these ideas in "The Vengeance of the Goddess Diana" is no more fully worked out than in "Avolio" itself, save that the expatiation of them in the revised poem suggests their importance and relevance to him.[2]

The "rewritten and amended" piece is not much of an improvement over the earlier version. Several critics—Whipple and a reviewer in the *Aldine*, among them—liked it; but the same general objections may be levied against the work in both stages of its development. It is too derivative in form, character, and technique. If Morris' "The Lady of the Land" appeared too late for Hayne to use, the same cannot be said about the poetry of Chaucer, Spenser, Tennyson, and Poe. As for Keats, the example of his "Lamia" may be said to be germinal in this instance, and Leigh Hunt provided the basis for the narrative itself. Altogether, Hayne's illustrious predecessors had offered him too much to assimilate in 1859. Sixteen years later, Hayne was a much more mature poet; but the poem was already molded, and he could not make fundamental changes in it without writing a different poem. That he could not and did not wish to do.

III *Other Narrative Poems*

Both "Frida and Her Poet" (*Southern Magazine*, June, 1873) and "The Visit of Mahmoud Ben Suleim to Paradise" (*Independent*, March 4, 1875) tell tales which demonstrate themes appealing to Hayne—the immortality of romantic love in the first poem and true morality in the second. Neither narrative offers much in the way of a strongly localized scene or highly particularized characters, but "Ben Suleim" remains of interest because it expresses rather well Hayne's own ideas about the relationship between right living and heavenly rewards. Originally called "Abou Ben Adhem's Visit to Paradise," the poem reveals a further debt to Leigh Hunt in its general ethical view. The framework is that of a dialogue. In the beginning Ben Suleim and a "brother sage" discourse on the "Past of Man" and seek knowledge of who "in Heaven and who in Hell" dwell now in "endless bliss or bale." The burden is on Ben Suleim, who tells of a "vision of eternity" in which he visited "Paradise" and held colloquy there with a "Fair Seraph" about those souls who have been translated to "Aidenn." Thus the dialogue moves from the two sages to Suleim and the angel and ends there.

The old man discovers in his dream that appearances are deceitful and that men who had in life seemed the most pious and righteous had not been so or had indeed been too zealous. Ibn Becár, for example, a man whose "righteous zeal burned hotly in his face," maintained "on his neighbor's ways so keen an eye" that "he lost at length his own straight course thereby." And Hafiz, known for his gifts to "general charities," nevertheless turned the "perishing beggar from his door" and wrung from "friendless widows" their "last crusts." These souls did not abide in Heaven. Wassaf, "the blameless teacher," was there in the "humblest sphere" because his virtue was a purely "negative" one. Not so with Saädi, the camel-smith, and Agha, "half tiger and half man," both of whom spent their lives trying to control their passions and conquer their sins. Their "weary" souls were allowed "to quaff the founts of balm." The seraph concludes:

> Would'st know the true believer? *He* is one
> Whose faith in deeds shines perfect as the sun.
> *His soul, a shaft feathered by works of grace,*
> *Death, the grim archer, launches forth in space;*
> *It cleaves the clouds, o'ershoots the vaporous wall*
> *That waves 'twixt earth and heaven its mystic pall,*
> *To light, at last, unerring, strong and fleet,*
> *In the deep calm which lies at Allah's feet!*

So it is with Hunt's Abou Ben Adhem, one whose name leads all the rest in the "book of gold" because he loves his "fellow-men."

These are precepts which Hayne tried to apply in his own life, and they have the ring of sincerity for that reason. He has also been fortunate in this instance in the management of the heroic couplets he has adopted as his measure. The poem achieves a sense of movement and rhythm not found in the other narratives in this volume. Moreover, the diction is not so affectedly poetic or overlaid with archaisms as to distract the reader's attention from the ideas being expressed. The dialogue is in itself an appropriate form for the treatment of these ideas; and, in the combination of all these factors, Hayne has created a philosophical narrative whose basic integrity may be respected after the passing of a century. In this sense at least and for its revelation of the poet's mind and heart, "The Visit of Mahmoud Ben Suleim to Paradise" deserves to rank among Hayne's better efforts in this genre.

IV *Lyrics*

The nature poems, the elegy on Timrod, the personal pieces, and the sonnets represent Hayne's verse in the rest of the collection. They are discussed here in reverse order so that the nature poems, Hayne's chief contribution to this volume, are treated last. Such an arrangement is, of course, arbitrary, for some of the sonnets or personal pieces may be viewed as nature poems and vice versa. Such classification does, however, suggest something about the scope of the poetry and its relationship to the poet's other work.

Several of the sonnets—"After the Tornado" and "As One Who Strays From Out Some Shadowy Glade"—deal with nature and personal matters, "a tremendous convulsion of the elements" and the poet's separation from "the populous city's life and light," respectively. "After the Tornado," published by the *Atlantic* in March, 1875, is particularly worthy of note:

> Last eve the earth was calm, the heavens were clear;
> A peaceful glory crowned the waning west,
> And yonder distant mountain's hoary crest
> The semblance of a silvery robe did wear,
> Shot through with moon-wrought tissues; far and near
> Wood, rivulet, field—all Nature's face—expressed
> The haunting presence of enchanted rest.
> One twilight star shone like a blissful tear,
> Unshed. But now, what ravage in a night!
> Yon mountain height fades in its cloud-girt pall;
> The prostrate wood lies smirched with rain and mire;
> Through the shorn fields the brook whirls, wild and
>   white;
> While o'er the turbulent waste, and woodland fall,
> Glares the red sunrise, blurred with mists of fire!

There are not so many personal poems in this collection as in the previous one. There is, for example, no verse addressed to his son; and Minna Hayne is less frequently the subject of his work, though "A Thousand Years from Now," a piece which begins with a suggestion of prophecy, ends on the note of the immortality of the love between the poet and his wife:

> But hearts like ours can ne'er forget,
> And though we know not *where*, nor *how*,
> Our conscious love shall blossom yet,
> A thousand years from now!

Hayne's own situation is seldom a topic in this book. The most poignant piece of this sort is perhaps "My Daughter," a wistful little lyric about a child he did not have:

> And yet she only lives for me
> In golden realms of fantasie,
> A creature born of air and beam,
> The delicate darling of a dream.

"By the Grave of Henry Timrod," called by Hayne his "In Memoriam," was written in January, 1874; and, after having been rejected by the *Atlantic* and the *Southern Magazine,* it was purchased for twenty-five dollars by Moses Coit Tyler of the *Christian Union* and was printed in the issue for June 10 (*Letters,* 331 ff.). Composed "not so much with ink," Hayne wrote Tyler, "as with *heart's blood,*" this piece, despite a more subjective view and expression of the subject, is a more impressive memorial to the dead poet than "Under the Pine."

Taking a traditional stance over the grave of his friend in Trinity Churchyard, Columbia, South Carolina, Hayne remembers their last meeting in September, 1867, in the context of his failure to recognize that Timrod was dying.

> My soul was blind; fear had not touched her sight
> To awful vision; so I bade thee go,
> Careless, and tranquil as that treacherous morn;
> Nor dreamed how soon the blight
> Of long-implanted seeds of care would throw
> Their nightshade flowers above the springing corn.

Returning to the present at his friend's "neglected" grave, he muses on the coldness of that "strange land—thy birth place and thy tomb" until he realizes that Timrod's spirit is not "here": "Death gave thee wings, and lo! thou hast soared above / All human utterance and all finite thought." At this moment, a "cordial sunbeam" breaks the clouds and shines on the "grave's head" and, with a "birdsong half divine," provides "an omen and a sign":

> In the bird's song an omen *his* must live!
>   In the warm glittering of that golden beam,
> A sign his soul's majestic hopes survive,
>   Raised to fruition o'er life's weary dream.
>   So now I leave him, low, yet restful here;
> So now I leave him, high-exalted, far
>   Beyond all memory of earth's guilt or guile;
>   Hark! 'tis his voice of cheer,
> Dropping, methinks, from some mysterious star;
>   His face I see, and on his face—a smile!

Here is Hayne at his best and worst. In terms of the poem's thought and development, the first seven lines of the last stanza are meaningful, appropriate, and right; indeed, in the treatment of the sunbeam and the bird's song, Hayne, though he despised Whitman's poetry, is doing in a minor way what the older poet had done on a larger scale a few years earlier with the lilac, star, and bird in "When Lilacs Last in the Dooryard Bloom'd."[3] But the last three lines, in idea if not in diction, destroy the quality of the effect the poem is on the verge of achieving. Even if such poetic terms as "hark" and "methinks" are taken for granted on the basis of nineteenth-century literary usage, there should be no place in this elegy for a "voice of cheer" to drop suddenly from any star, mysterious or otherwise; or for this experience to conjure up in the mind of his brother artist a vision of the smiling face of the dead poet! Such a conclusion weakens the effect of the whole poem.

Aside from this lapse, the poem is a moving if not quite "noble" (as Tyler characterized it) tribute to Timrod and their friendship. Less formal in tone and texture and more immediate in the emotion expressed than "Under the Pine," Hayne comes close to making "By the Grave of Henry Timrod" an artistic endeavor "worthy" of a "sad, but most *impressive theme.*"

The nature lyrics, all dealing in one way or another with the poet's surroundings at Copse Hill and many published first in the *Atlantic Monthly,* were written over a two-year period beginning in the late winter of 1872. The first poem was called "Aspects of the Pines" and became his initial postwar contribution to the *Atlantic* when Howells accepted it in March, 1872, and printed it in the September issue. A picture in five quatrains of the pines at morning, noon, afternoon, sunset, and twilight, the view of nature offered— despite the nearness of the pines in question in a "superb pine forest" opposite Copse Hill—is somewhat Romantic, though some esthetic distance is achieved through the adoption of an omniscient point of view:

> Tall, sombre, grim, against the morning sky
> They rise, scarce touched by melancholy airs,
> Which stir the fadeless foliage dreamfully,
> As if from realms of mystical despairs.

The tone of the poem is marred, as Howells maintained, by the "prettyness" of the last stanza:

> Till every lock is luminous—gently float,
> Fraught with hale odors up the heavens afar
> To faint when Twilight on her virginal throat
> Wears for a gem the tremulous vesper star.

Hayne, however, defended himself against Howells' criticism, pointing out in a letter of September 10, 1872, to Mrs. Preston, that he had "*purposely* introduced that 'Twilight' image to *relieve* the *dark* colors elsewhere employed in a realistic picture of Nature." Nevertheless, Hayne was encouraged by Howells' general opinion of "Aspects" to begin immediately to write more verse on his observations of natural life in his neighborhood.

And Howells rose to the occasion. He accepted six more poems of this type and rejected, among others, only two of any importance —"In the Pine Barrens" and "Midsummer in the South"—both of which were shortly thereafter published in other periodicals. Howells printed "Forest Pictures. Morning" in December, 1872; "The Voice in the Pines" in January, 1873; "The Wood Lake" in April,

1873; "Golden Dell" in October, 1873; "The Woodland" in October, 1874; and "Visit of the Wrens" in December, 1874.

"Forest Pictures. Morning" is a rather conventional piece in the Wordsworth-Bryant school of nature poetry, though the diction, with its "purpling hills" and "murmurous rills," smacks more of Bryant's style than of Wordsworth's language of men. But even in a world of "sylvan shades" and "solemn silences" the mockingbird sings and

> Shy forms about the greenery, out and in,
>   Flit 'neath the broadening glories of the morn;
> The squirrel—that quaint sylvan harlequin—
>   Mounts the tall trunks; while swift as lightning, born
> Of summer mists, from tangled vine and tree
> Dart the dove's pinions, pulsing vividly
> Down the dense glades, till glimmering far and gray
> The dusky vision softly melts away!

All this and more is viewed by a speaker to whose "fevered spirit" comes "peace" as his senses mark the sights and sounds of the "deer-hound's mellow tongue," the "huntsman's horn," and a vision of "Heaven's calm infinity" from the vantage point of a "pine clad height." If not new or original, the idea is clear: nature brings peace and possibility of communion with infinity.

As its title suggests, "The Voice in the Pines" is related to "Aspects of the Pines." "I've just been walking under my favorite pine trees," Hayne wrote Mrs. Preston on September 15, 1872, "adding some touches here & there to a little poem, designed as a sort of sequel, or a twin picture to 'Aspects of the Pines.' . . . They came to me unbidden, as it were, and almost set themselves to music. Are they good? I cannot tell." "The Voice in the Pines" is a more subjective rendering of the poet's response to the grove opposite his home than its predecessor. A speaker in the poem describes a "bodiless voice" coming from the trees:

> What voice is this? what low and solemn tone,
>   Which, though all wings of all the winds seem furled,
> Nor even the zephyr's fairy flute is blown,
> Makes thus forever its mysterious moan
>   From out the whispering pine-tops' shadowy world?

Are the "antique tales" about dryads true, the speaker wonders, or can it be that some "baffled ocean-spirit" has become lost and "yearns for the sharp, sweet kisses of the sea?":

> Whate'er the spell, I hearken and am dumb,
>   Dream-touched, and musing in the tranquil morn;
> All woodland sounds—the pheasant's gusty drum,
> The mockbird's fugue, the droning insect's hum—
>   Scarce heard for that strange, sorrowful voice forlorn!
>
> Beneath the drowsèd sense, from deep to deep
>   Of spiritual life its mournful minor flows,
> Streamlike, with pensive tide, whose currents keep
> Low murmuring 'twixt the bounds of grief and sleep,
>   Yet locked for aye from sleep's divine repose.

And thus the voice of nature in the voice in the pines enchants the speaker until, in the serene and dreamlike mood which follows, he penetrates momentarily the surface of consciousness and sees into the "spiritual life." Without pushing the parallels too far or too exactly, echoes of "Tintern Abbey" may be heard here, and anticipations of "The Marshes of Glynn" (especially in the concluding passages) may be observed. Despite his question to Mrs. Preston about the merit of the verses, Hayne certainly thought well of them since he placed "The Voice in the Pines" at the head of all the nature poems in the volume.

The remaining nature poems from the *Atlantic* treat nature generally in a conventional, Romantic way. "The Wood Lake" (called "The Solitary Lake" in *The Mountain of the Lovers*) and "Golden Dell" are descriptive in character and offer a minimum of moral content. "The Woodland" (changed to "The Woodland Phases" in the collection) takes up Wordsworth's theme of "one impulse from a vernal wood," and "Visit of the Wrens" develops a variation of that theme. But each of these pieces has its individual touches. "The Solitary Lake" captures an experience in which mood and atmosphere are evoked and particularized at the same time from the "delicate mists of morning" when, amidst the "fitful, murmurous sighs" of the rising "west wind," the lake ripples and the vapors

melt away until, "flushed by morning's primrose-red," the day
arrives:

> With brightening morn the mockbird's lay
> Grows stronger, mellower; far away
> 'Mid dusky reeds, which even the noon
> Lights not, the lonely-hearted loon
> Makes answer, her shrill music shorn
> Of half its sadness; day, full-born,
> Doth rout all sounds and sights forlorn.

The "Golden Dell," a "sweet, secluded place" offers hints of
early spring (and Paradise) in the song of mockingbird, thrush, and
wren; in the "clear stream" which flows " 'twixt banks of violet and
rose"; and in the jasmine, the "half-grown woodbine flowers." And
"O'er purpling rows of wild-wood peas, / So blandly borne, the
droning bees / Still suck their honeyed cores at ease. . . ."

"The Woodland Phases" despite its obvious debt to Wordsworth's
"The Tables Turned" reaches a different conclusion:

> The wild bird's strain, the breezy spray—
>> Each hour with sure earth-changes rife—
> Hints more than all the sages say,
>> Or poets sing of death and life.
>
> For, truths half drawn from Nature's breast,
>> Through subtlest types of form and tone,
> Outweigh what man, at most, hath guessed
>> While heeding his own heart alone.
>
> And midway, betwixt heaven and us,
>> Stands Nature, in her fadeless grace,
> Still pointing to our Father's house,
>> His glory on her mystic face.

Though the "Visit of the Wrens" leads the poet to speculate in
a Bryant-like way on the meaning of this experience, he does not
offer Bryant's moral warmed over. Indeed, after some excellent
description of his "tiny, springtide friends" and their labors of
building a nest and tending it, he muses on the implications of the
visit and on the example of the birds themselves. Suppose, he re-

flects, that the birds fail to return another spring: "at least the good ye brought,/The delicate charms for eye and thought/Survives."

> . . . not the less
> Your simple drama shall impress
> Fancy and heart, thus acted o'er
> Toward each small issue, as of yore,
> With sun and wind and skies of blue
> To witness, wondering, all you do,
> Because your happy toil and mirth
> May be of fine, ideal birth;
> Because each quick, impulsive note
> May thrill a visionary throat,
> Each flash of glancing wing and eye
> Be gleams of vivid fantasy;
> Since whatsoe'er of form and tone
> A past reality hath known,
> Most charming unto soul and sense,
> But wins that subtle effluence,
> That spiritual air which softly clings
> About all sweet and vanished things,
> Causing a bygone joy to be
> Vital as actuality,
> Yet with each earthlier tint or trace
> Lost in a pure, ethereal grace!

If not of the scope of Whitman's thought and vision in his bird poems or of the distinction of concentration and imagery of Emily Dickinson's, this lyric has its own quality; but its limitations are more readily apparent in the context of such a comparison. Hayne's poetic response to the visit of the wrens, then, may be more clearly judged in the light of Whitman's response to the two birds from Alabama or of Miss Dickinson's to the hummingbird in the bush.[4]

Of the nature pieces not published in the *Atlantic*, two merit brief examination. "In the Pine Barrens. Sunset," which appeared in the *Independent* for April 3, 1873, is something of a companion piece in idea at least to "Forest Pictures. Morning." A descriptive idyl of sunset in the barrens as it is viewed by a speaker who notes the dying wind and the dying day and the clouds "massed on the marvellous heaven in splendid pyres," the poem contains a memorable image of "blasted," "bodeful" pines:

> One stalwart hill his stern defiant crest
> > Boldly against the horizon line uprears,
> His blasted Pines, smit by the fiery West,
> > Uptowering rank on rank, like Titan spears;

> Fantastic, bodeful, o'er the rock-strewn ground
> > Casting grim shades beyond the hill slope riven,
> Which mock the loftier shafts, keen, lustre-crowned
> > And raised as if to storm the courts of Heaven!

"Midsummer in the South" (*Christian Union*, May 14, 1873) is developed in a series of four statements by a speaker: "I love Queen August's stately sway"; "I love midsummer's azure deep"; "I love midsummer uplands, free"; and "I love midsummer sunsets, rolled." Queen August bears "stately sway" over "fragrant south winds" and the "rare midsummer dream" that lies in "Nature's eyes" and whose "witchery broods o'er earth and skies." The clouds lie entranced on "midsummer's azure deep." The uplands provide the speaker with a place to see and hear, "Where, nested warm in yellowing grass, / I hear the swift-winged partridge pass, / With whirr and boom of gusty flight, / Across the broad heath's treeless height." And the midsummer sunsets with their "waves of gold" and "blazing crests of billowy fire" lead him to a statement which is a modification of a theme sounded near the end of "Visit of the Wrens":

> In gentler mood I love to mark
> The slow gradations of the dark;
> Till, lo! from Orient's mists withdrawn,
> Hail! to the Moon's resplendent dawn . . .
> She bathes the rescued world in light,
> So that, albeit my Summer's Day
> Erewhile did breathe its life away,
> Methinks, whate'er its hours had won
> Of beauty, born from shade and sun,
> Hath not perchance so wholly died,
> But o'er the moonlight's silvery tide
> Comes back, sublimed and purified!

Other poems in *The Mountain of the Lovers* may be mentioned —"Violets," the "fairy flowers" whose perfume induces "strange shades of half forgotten hours"; "Ariel," a poetic sketch of a beau-

tiful woman based on one of Hayne's favorite Shakespearean characters; "The Cloud-Star," a fable which stimulated Lanier to write
on May 23, 1874: "I am charmed with it, and am not sure but I
shall come presently to think it the strongest thing you have done";
and "Lucifer's Deputy," one of Hayne's few humorous poems and a
jeu d'esprit sent to Tyler in April, 1874, as a "good natured sarcasm
upon mediaëval credulity." But the poems already discussed adequately represent Hayne's work in *The Mountain of the Lovers* and
may be taken as fair examples of his mature output in 1875.

V *Critical Response*

The reviews of *The Mountain of the Lovers* were generally favorable.[5] The critics noted the Southern qualities in the poetry and
almost without exception characterized Hayne as the "Poet of the
South." Many reviewers preferred the lyrics to the poems of tradition, though Whipple and one or two others spoke well of both
types; and the nature poems received unqualified endorsement.
Several pointed out that intense feeling predominated over intellectual strength, and Whipple suggested that "something of the
spirit of Crabbe" might be infused in the work. A reviewer in
Appletons' Journal commented without unfavorable implication that
Hayne declined "to recognize an obligation . . . 'to set the crooked
straight,' to storm the soul with passionate lyrics, or to grope with
morbid curiosity amid the inner recesses of the human heart.
Enough for him," he continued, "to delineate the scenes and interpret the moods of Nature, and to reveal to the reader a few of those
melodies which communion with Nature has awakened in his
heart." Quite a few of the critics (among them Maurice Thompson
and James Barron Hope, poets themselves) praised the sonnets and
ranked Hayne as one of the best sonneteers in America. Finally,
several thought that *The Mountain of the Lovers* was an advance
in Hayne's poetic development. Thompson, for example, observed
that it was a "more worthy volume" than *Legends and Lyrics* and
added that the author seemed "to be just finding his note and assuring himself of it"; and Whipple concluded that the collection was
Hayne's "best" one because it exhibited "his genius in the maturity
of its power."

Hayne himself, however, did not share all these opinions. He
regertted publishing "The Mountain of the Lovers," but he liked

the nature pieces. He was also aware of the shortcomings of some of the other poems in the volume, and he wrote Mrs. Preston on March 30, 1875, of his disappointment in not being able always to maintain his standards. "I am *forced* to write, *too often forced* to write for 'bread'; and the consequence is, that 'Pegasus' unwillingly weighted with harness, plays me many a wretched prank. . . . I have had my name (continually) attached to verses which fall infinitely below the standard every true Poet of our generation should practically hold in view. God pity and forgive me! *He* only knows what I have had to *endure.*"[6]

Despite the truth of these remarks, there is good work in *The Mountain of the Lovers*. The narrative poems, with the possible exception of "Mahmoud Ben Suleim," are not successful, but neither are they complete failures. And the nature lyrics are an advance over his earlier work, as Howells quickly indicated by accepting so many for the *Atlantic*; moreover, these pieces, as both Anderson and Hubbell have pointed out, influenced Lanier to turn to the Southern scene of his own day. As a whole, *The Mountain of the Lovers* does not compare favorably with *Legends and Lyrics* in scope or variety or quality; but it is not an unworthy collection. Had Hayne been more patient and discriminating, he might have waited another year or two and published a volume of lyrics (he actually planned such a book in 1876) which might have established him firmly as an important, contemporary American lyrist. Lowell's earlier advice to him "to sift" and aim for "quality" by reducing the quantity of work had, for a variety of reasons, not been considered so carefully in *The Mountain of the Lovers*.

CHAPTER 5

Poems, Complete Edition, 1882

A YEAR and a half after the publication of *The Mountain of the Lovers*, Hayne had another volume of poems ready for the press. Composed of verses "wholly miscellaneous & lyrical," this collection was never issued, though several publishers gave it serious consideration. Henry Holt, for example, was interested enough after discussing the proposed volume with Moses Coit Tyler (who, along with E. C. Stedman, had been commissioned by Hayne to present his manuscript to various New York houses) to suggest that he might bring out a book selected from the entire range of Hayne's poetic output if the copyright was assigned to his firm. Hayne was willing to release the copyright if necessary, but he was reluctant to do so at the time, for another friend, John Garland James, was seeking ways and means of getting a complete edition of Hayne's work before the public. The negotiations with Holt, however, ended unsuccessfully in December, 1878; two years later, after James had secured almost two hundred subscribers, the Boston firm of D. Lothrop agreed to bring out a complete edition at its own risk.

Poems of Paul Hamilton Hayne, Complete Edition, appeared in October, 1882, in several bindings and printed on heavy gilt-edged paper with a biographical sketch by Mrs. Preston and sixty-one illustrations. Hayne thought that Lothrop had produced an "*exceedingly handsome book,*" but he was so disturbed by the numerous typographical errors and by several omissions that he had an errata sheet sent to his friends and fellow poets; for, as he wrote Tyler on December 11, 1882, "it would *never do* for the *general public* to imagine the '*Edition incorrect*', else it would prevent sale, & the possibility of a 2nd edition. . . . *After* all," he concluded, "the *mistakes* will only attract the notice of careful & scholarly readers!!"[1]

The Complete Edition, of course, is not really complete even to 1882. It contains the poet's own selection of his work from previous volumes to which he added much that he had written from 1875 to the summer of 1882. Though his early verse is carefully winnowed, a number of pieces were retained from his first two books, chiefly as they had appeared in *Avolio,* the first collected edition. Seventeen war poems are included, though few had been collected before. All save a sonnet on William Morris are reprinted from *Legends and Lyrics. The Mountain of the Lovers* is also reprinted with little change, for only two sonnets are omitted. The remainder of the edition, with few exceptions, is composed of uncollected poems written and published since *The Mountain of the Lovers* had appeared in 1875. Despite Hayne's arrangement of these pieces under three headings—"Later Poems," "Humorous Poems," and "Poems for Children"—there are only seven humorous pieces and thirty for children. Consequently, the bulk of the later work is composed of lyrics in great variety and profusion.

The early verse which appears in the Complete Edition suggests adequately enough Hayne's accomplishment as a "youthful" poet. "My Father," "The Will and the Wing," and the sonnets on Shelley and October are surely among the best pieces appearing in *Poems,* and the "Ode to Sleep" is the best long poem, just as "Great Poets and Small," "My Study," and "To W. H. H." represent the poet's achievement as a sonneteer in *Sonnets, and Other Poems.* All of these works, variously changed or revised, had been reprinted in *Avolio.* "My Father," for example, was drastically cut when it was reprinted and "To W. H. H." in 1882 brings together two early sonnets addressed to Will Hayne; but only minor changes in diction and punctuation were made in the other pieces, a general practice also followed in preparing them for their final appearance in the Complete Edition. Of the new verse in *Avolio,* a few sonnets are retained, "Avolio" itself (as it was later revised for *The Mountain of the Lovers* under the title of "The Vengeance of the Goddess Diana"), and two odes, "Nature the Consoler" and the occasional poem written for the Carolina Art Association in 1859.

The war poems give a general idea of Hayne's support of the Confederacy; but, in editing them for the Complete Edition, he sometimes toned down their passion and fervor (as in the case of "My Mother-Land," for example); and, by not including such ardent pieces as "The Kentucky Partisan" and "Butler's Proclamation," his "rebellious" sentiments appear less vehement than they actually were. He had no wish, of course, to revive old controversies in a book already subscribed for by many prominent Northerners and intended for distribution to readers throughout the country.[2] But the edition was, after all, a "complete" one; and he decided that his work would not be properly represented without some of the verse about various aspects of the Confederacy and about the war itself.

The reprinting in the Complete Edition of almost all of the poems in *Legends and Lyrics* and *The Mountain of the Lovers* clearly illustrates Hayne's own critical view and that of his contemporaries that his reputation prior to 1882 rested largely on these collections. That there is little revision between printing in these works and in the Complete Edition confirms Hayne's general attitude toward "burnishing" his verse. He not only felt that one could overdo revision, but he found such work less to his taste (he wrote Mrs. Preston on July 26, 1878) than composition itself: "My *own* most exquisite enjoyment derived from the visits of the Muse, has always been in the act of *conception* followed by swift *execution*. When the period of *correction* came, the duty of *labor limae*, I shrank from, and detested it! To the very *last*, I shall *hate* this *duty;* still a *duty* it unquestionably is!" He thought the "task" of preparing the text for the Complete Edition not only "incessant toil" but "somewhat humiliating," for he became aware of many "artistic shortcomings." Nevertheless, he went over the "entire 'Copy' " several times, his revision being confined chiefly to the first examination (and that to a slight polishing here and there rather than to a thoroughgoing alteration). In succeeding considerations he was concerned primarily with "arrangement" and with the "interpolation" of new poems into the text.

Indeed, this new work gives the Complete Edition an added dimension, for the book becomes not only a repository for Hayne's best work from the previous collections but a gathering together of new work published over a period of seven years. Thus, some of his most mature output in the way of lyrics, sonnets, ballads, memorials and occasional verse, pieces of a meditative and religious cast, and laureate-type statements in which he speaks as the poet of the South is thereby presented in one volume. This maturity is readily discernible in the better work in "Later Poems."

"Unveiled," "Muscadines," and "The Snow Messengers" are among the best long lyrics Hayne ever wrote.

I *"Unveiled"*

Dedicated by permission to William Cullen Bryant and purchased for fifty dollars by J. G. Holland for *Scribner's Monthly,* where it appeared in January, 1878, "Unveiled" is a long, irregular ode reminiscent in one or two passages of "Tintern Abbey," and it is also Wordsworthian in its general philosophical view of nature. The dominant figure in the early part of the poem is Nature, the "queenly mother" whose "influence fine . . . runs like Arcadian wine / Through all my being" and who prompts the poet to walk "the earth all-seeing." Thus he reports:

> . . . not her stateliest forms
> Alone engrossed me, nor her sounds of power;
> Mountains and oceans, and the rage of storms;
> Fierce cataracts hurled from awful steep to steep,
> Or, the gray water-spouts, that whirling tower
> Along the darkened bosom of the deep;
> But all fair, fairy forms; all vital things,
> That breathe or blossom 'midst our bounteous springs;
>> In sylvan nooks rejoicingly I met
>> The wild rose and the violet;
> On dewy hill-slopes pausing, fondly talked
>> With the coy wind-flower, and the grasses brown,
>> That in a subtle language of their own
>> (Caught from the spirits of the wandering breeze),
>> Quaintly responded; while the heavens looked down
>>> As graciously on these
>> Titania growths, as on sublimer shapes
>> Of century-moulded continents, that bemock
>> Alike the earthquake's and the billows' shock
>> By Orient inlands and cold ocean capes!

He "worships" the "giant constellations," "long mosses," "virginal vines," "networks of golden ferns," and concludes that "No life is trivial, no creation small!" His "spiritual ear" hears Nature's "multitudinous voices" and "every tiniest trill of sound." The "lay" of the mockingbird and the thrush lead him to suspect

remoter meanings; the far tone
Of ante-natal music faintly blown
From out the misted realms of memory;
The pathos and the passion of a dream;
Or, broken fugues of a diviner tongue
That e'er hath chanted, since our earth was young,
And o'er her peace-enamored solitudes
The stars of morning sung!

Bryant remarked on the "genuine poetic enthusiasm" of the piece in a letter of November 1, 1877, to Hayne; and Dr. Holland praised it on September 10 in unequivocal terms: "This is much the best, largest, most strongly and evenly sustained piece of work I have ever seen from your hand. I do not know when I can publish it. It is too long, really, for my use, but I cannot send it back to you." Hayne himself thought well of it, though he had, as he wrote Mrs. Preston on October 21, once entertained some doubts about it— "the *vast interval* between *conception* & *execution*, struck me like a mental & spiritual *chill*"—but, when he revised the poem later, he concluded that it was "among the best" he had ever "penned."

Hayne's equanimity about the poem, however, was shaken a few months later when Bayard Taylor commented that it wanted "distinctness" in conception and development. "There is the *Substance* of a noble poem in it," he wrote Hayne on January 28, 1878, "but the Key-stone of an arch is lacking." Stedman, on the other hand, praised the ode and restored Hayne's faith. Years later, in an exchange of letters with Andrew Adgate Lipscomb, Hayne remarked on November 14, 1884, that he had reached his "highest water mark" in "Unveiled." In response, Lipscomb observed on November 18 that he considered the piece "upper-most among all your poems as to the individuation of Nature's power over the spiritual senses and the entire subserviency of sense-impressions to the higher subjectiveness." It has, he added on December 3, "a closer unity and . . . is more congruous with itself than the grand ode by Wordsworth." This verdict is the partial one of a friend, but "Unveiled," despite the justice of Taylor's strictures, is nevertheless one of Hayne's best poems. The idea is neither new nor adequately elaborated, and the form is not fully organic in its function; but the sonority of expression and the mystical reverence for nature in this ode are impressive and not unworthy of the Romantic tradition in which it is written.

II "*Muscadines*"

"Muscadines," written about a year earlier than "Unveiled," was published in *Harper's Monthly* in December, 1876. Also an irregular ode, "Muscadines" deals, at least in its beginning and ending, more directly with the Southern scene than does "Unveiled." However, the vision of Arcadian nature in the middle part leads the reader to forget too readily the substance of the locale in the never-never land of fauns and naiads conjured up by the grape.

Based on the old envelope narrative structure in which a narrator is introduced within a particular background, has a dream or vision which transports him to a different and often exotic world, and returns at the end to the familiar setting of the beginning, "Muscadines" follows the pattern without modification. In "sober September," amidst the "autumnal leaves" of a forest, the narrator wanders "through shade and shine" until he marks "the temperate tide/ Purpled by shadows of the Muscadine":

> Reclining there at languid length I sank,
> One idle hand outstretched beyond the bank,
>   With careless grasp
> The sumptuous globes of these rare grapes to clasp.
> Ah! how the ripened wild fruit of the South
>   Melted upon my mouth!
> Its magic juices through each captured vein
>   Rose to the yielding brain,
> Till, like the hero of an old romance,
> Caught by the fays, my spirit lapsed away,
> Lost to the sights and sounds of mortal day.

Then, as though "stirred by some new being's wondrous dawn," the narrator in a trancelike state sees and hears a "multitudinous company of . . . strange forms and faces" gliding through the "forest coverts." The dancers form a line

> Down the deep glade—above the shifting lights,
> Through massive tree-boles, on majestic heights;
>   The blossoming turf thereunder,
>   Whence, fair and fine,
> Twinkling like stars that hasten to be drawn
>   Close to the breast of dawn,

Shone, with their blue veins pulsing fleet,
        Innumerable feet,
White as the splendors of the milky way,
Yet rosy warm as opening tropic day,
With lithe, free limbs of curvature divine,
And dazzling bosoms of unveilèd glow,
Save where the long, ethereal tresses stray
Across their unimaginable snow.

They pass "vision-like" before him, a "Dryad coy," a "frank-faced Oread," fauns and satyrs, a "lightsome and slim" naiad, until he "seemed, in sooth . . . to have wandered, joyful, back/ Along the paths, beneath the crystal sky/ Of long, long-perished Arcady." The naiad strikes him:

O'er her sloped shoulders and the pure pink bud
Of either virginal breast is richly rolled
        (O rare, miraculous flood!)
The torrent of her freed locks' shimmering gold,
Through which the gleams of rainbow-colored shells,
And pearls of moon-like radiance flash and float
        Round her immaculate throat.

Clothed in her beauty only wandered she,
'Mid the moist herbage to the streamlet's edge,
Where, girt by silvery rushes and brown sedge,
She faded slowly, slowly, as a star
Fades in the gloaming, on the bosom bowed
        Of some half-luminous cloud,
Above the wan, waste waters of the sea.

As the vision fades, the narrator falls into a deep "oblivious" sleep from which he only awakens at twilight:

At length the wind of evening, keenly chill,
Swept round the darkening hill;
Then throbbed the rush of hurried wings o'erhead,
Blent with aerial murmurs of the pine,
Just whispering twilight. On my brow the dew
Dropped softly, and I woke to all the low,
Strange sounds of twilight woods that come and go
So fitfully; and o'er the sun's decline,
Through the green foliage flickering high,

Beheld, with dreamy eye,
Sweet Venus glittering in the stainless blue.

. . . .

Thus the day closed whereon I drank the wine—
The liquid magic of the Muscadine.

Returning to the reality of the woods of the present, the narrator
reasserts the "magic" of the Southern grape, and the poem ends
where it began. In the meanwhile, it has transported reader and
poet alike to an older mythical world where all is Elysian light and
airy fantasy.

Despite conventional idea, structure, and diction, this ode possesses a quality which mitigates its conventionality. Its musical flow
brings to mind parts of the *Faerie Queene,* the odes of Keats (especially the one to the nightingale), a lyric or two of Poe, and the
songs of Tennyson; but the music is not derivative in the sense that
it appears to come from any one of these masters. It is neither the
numbers which lull a gentle knight to "slumber soft" in the house
of Morpheus, nor those which charm "magic casements . . . in faery
lands forlorn," nor those which suggest a "wild weird clime . . . Out
of Space—Out of Time," nor even those which bring "sweet sleep
down from the blissful skies." It is rather Hayne's own music; born
of his predecessors perhaps, its heritage is so well absorbed that it
bears Hayne's stamp, not theirs. As Thompson proclaimed, too
enthusiastically, in a letter to Hayne of December 8, 1876: "No
one else could have written it."

Edgar Fawcett and Moses Coit Tyler also congratulated Hayne
on the poem. Tyler read it aloud and reported in a letter of June
20, 1877, that he "was borne up to a high excitement & pleasure by
its magnificence—its gorgeous imagery, its opulence of diction, its
passion, its delicate mystical & profound suggestiveness," and in
subsequent letters he usually referred to the piece as the "immortal
'Muscadines.'" The chief accolade, as far as Hayne was concerned,
came from Swinburne, with whom he had corresponded for over a
year. The British poet wrote that the verses were "so full of the
color & fragrance & health of the beauty they describe that they
make one long to enjoy these also in person" (*Letters*, 336). It is
no wonder, then, that Hayne thought well enough of "Muscadines"
to make it in the late 1870's the title piece of a proposed collection

of lyrics and in 1882 to include it immediately after "Unveiled" in the Complete Edition.

III *"The Snow Messengers"*

Called first "Snow in the South" and occasioned by a "notable snow-storm" of November 12, 1879, the poem soon became a means of embodying Hayne's impressions of Northern scenery and people and, especially, of those friends who had greeted him and his wife so hospitably on their recent visit to New York and New England. Longfellow and Whittier, having been particularly kind and for some years having served him as benevolent literary well-wishers and models, were selected for special attention in the dedication and in "pen portraits." With such subject matter and themes, the poem was immediately accepted by *Harper's Monthly* and published in March, 1880.

Unlike "Muscadines" and "Unveiled" in its iambic quatrains rhyming *aabb*, "The Snow Messengers" resembles the former in structure at least, for it too follows the general envelope pattern of the earlier piece. Similar views of nature are manifested in all three poems, but the chief note of the last one is admiration and affection for the two Northern poets—a gesture of reconciliation in itself coming as it does from the poet laureate of the South. The celebration of this theme and the use to which nature is put distinguish this piece from the other two nature lyrics.

The poem opens with the narrator looking out on the pines as the snow falls silently. He makes a snowball from the flakes falling on his window sill and remembers the "fair past." "Ariel fancy" takes him "once more" to the mountains, pastures, farms, lakes, and dells of New England; and, as he commands fancy's "wing" to stay "near northern hearts and homes," the narrator notes that he still cherishes the South:

> But a new epoch greets us; with it blends
> The voice of ancient foes now changed to friends.
> Ah! who would friendship's outstretched hand despise,
> Or mock the kindling light in generous eyes?

From this statement of reconciliation, he moves directly to the portrait of the "Quaker-poet" as artist, philosopher, moralist, and

man: "our pure, hale-minded Cowper of the West." Then Longfellow receives his share of praise as poet and as "cordial prince of
kindly men." The portraits done, the speaker muses:

> Still are ye near me, vivid, actual still,
> Here in my lonely fastness on the hill;
> Nor can ye wane till cold my life-blood flows,
> And fancy fades in feeling's last repose.

Suddenly he returns to the reality of the moment when the snow
is still falling, and he recapitulates briefly the power of the snow
messengers from the North whose "coldness thrills like flame";

> Yes, falling still, while fond remembrance stirs
> In these wan-faced, unwonted messengers.
> Dumb storm! outpour your arctic heart's desire!
> Your flakes to me seem flushed with fairy fire!

Nature in this poem as represented by the snow is a means of
removing the narrator in spirit to a region of "northern hearts and
homes." Transported through "tireless fancy" to New England, he
sees Whittier as a man concerned with the "hard problems of our
mortal lot" and yet as one who enjoys the humble pleasures of his
own "hearth-stone." Indeed, in the lines describing Whittier relaxing
at home with his dog and cat (in this bit of detail one senses a
certain kinship to Whittier's own *Snow-Bound*), Hayne draws on
the experiences of his recent visit at Oak Knoll. The sketch of Longfellow, despite his fondness for "homeliest thoughts and homeliest
things" is not, however, rendered in such homely detail. It is Longfellow the "Arcadian" poet and gracious gentleman whose serenity
of spirit has captured the author's interest.

Both Whittier and Longfellow wrote Hayne expressing their
appreciation of the honor he had done them. Edgar Fawcett wrote
on March 8, 1880, that he thought the poem "full of tender, aerial
fantasies, and a beautiful panegyrical tribute to those whose song
you venerate." Hayne himself thought that it was "among his best,"
though, when he saw the poem in *Harper's*, he was "disappointed"
to find, so he acknowledged to Mrs. Preston on February 20, that
his "expression" had fallen below his "conception." The favorable
opinions of others, however, soon restored his faith in a work he
had taken "great trouble with."

As poetic art "The Snow Messengers" has less to offer than "Unveiled" or "Muscadines," but as literary history—particularly as a tribute of affection and esteem on the part of an unreconstructed Southern man of letters to two former antislavery Yankee poets—it is more significant than either of the other two lyrics.

IV *Shorter Lyrics*

There are many quotable brief lyrics in the Complete Edition— "The Dryad of the Pine," "The Pine's Mystery," "To a Bee," "The First Mocking-Bird in Spring," "Love's Autumn," "The Spirea," "Forest Quiet. (In the South.)," "The Mocking-Bird. (At Night.)," "The Inevitable Calm," "Hints of Spring. (Composed in Sickness.)," "The Fallen Pine-Cone," and "England," to mention only a few in the order they appear. For the most part, these are nature poems, though there are exceptions: one is addressed to Hayne's wife (and another treats her substantially but indirectly), whereas others deal with his personal situation and his love of beauty.

"Love's Autumn," for example, is a tribute to Mary Michel Hayne in a variation of the terza rima in which the rhyme runs *aab ccb dde ffe,* and so on. Written in 1880 when Hayne was fifty and Mrs. Hayne forty-nine and published in *Scribner's Monthly* for October, the piece exhibits the poet's mature and mellow passion:

> Thus, at each slow, but surely deepening sign
> Of life's decay, we will not, Sweet! repine,
> Nor greet its mellowing close with thankless tears;
>
> Love's spring was fair, love's summer brave and bland,
> But through love's autumn mist I view the land,
> The land of deathless summers yet to be;
>
> There, I behold thee, young again and bright,
> In a great flood of rare transfiguring light,
> But there as here, thou smilest, Love! on me!

Of all Hayne's personal poems, "England" is surely one of the most poignant. The epitome of everything he admired in the way of tradition and culture, England was always the land of his dreams. Prevented from going there before the Civil War by illness in the family and afterward by his own frail health and poverty, Hayne wrote his son on February 1, 1886, only six months before his death, that if any word were found engraved on his heart it would be "*England*." The poem itself celebrates this land of his father's love and race whose "humblest dust" is touched by "golden histories and majestic dreams" and whose "sacred places"—ivied temples, "castled homes," "opulent towns"—abound with marvels. More than anything else he "yearns" to "bow" before England's poets—"the laureate," Swinburne, and "other glorious minstrels"—who are "bound" to his life by "many a rhythmic tie." But, alas, he knows that this was not meant to be. "O'er dreary hills the gaunt pines moan and sigh;/ Pale grows my dream, pierced through by bodeful pain;/ England! I shall not see thee ere I die!"

The most important brief lyrics are those which deal with nature. "The Dyrad of the Pine," "The Pine's Mystery," and "The Fallen Pine-Cone" extol the "mysterious tree" within the "numberless, dim complexities" of whose cones are absorbed the sounds of "all winds that blow" as well as the "elemental virtues of all airs" and within whose "imprisoning bark" is "something rare" which makes "Elysian all the haunted place."[3] The enigmatic quality of the tree is suggested succinctly in the two stanzas of "The Pine's Mystery":

> Listen! the sombre foliage of the Pine,
>   A swart Gitana of the woodland trees,
> Is answering what we may but half divine,
>   To those soft whispers of the twilight breeze!
>
> Passion and mystery murmur through the leaves,
>   Passion and mystery, touched by deathless pain,
> Whose monotone of long, low anguish grieves
>   For something lost that shall not live again!

In contrast to the pine poems, "To a Bee" is in an Anacreontic vein modernized by a sensuous Romanticism. The bee, an erotic "mite," plunders where he will in nature's garden "from half-blown bud to flower all matron-fair." The jonquil and the "blossoming quince" "yield" to him their "delicate richness," and the jasmine offers its "petalled cup" to be drained. Now "honey-freighted," the "small epicurean" pauses for a moment to consider the other pleasures the world affords:

> A moment only. Soon your matchless flight
>   Cleaves the far blue; your elfin thunder booms
> In elfin echoes from yon glimmering height,
>   To fall and die amid these ravished blooms.

Then, in a final stanza, the poet relates his effort (and the bee's) to the Anacreontic tradition:

> Gone, like a vision! Yet, be sure that he
> > Hath only flown through lovelier flowers to stray,
> Anacreon's soul, thus prisoned in a bee,
> > Still sips and sings the springtide hours away! [4]

"The Spirea" and "Forest Quiet" deal with aspects of nature in the South. The first celebrates in *Harper's Bazar* for August 19, 1876, the "fair plant" whose stems are "veiled in white blossoms like a cloud/ Of daintiest bridal lace" and whose blossoms seem "half woven of moonshine's misty bars." The second, originally called "Summer Quiet (In the Southern Woods)" in *Scribner's Monthly* for June, 1877, describes that "sylvan silence" where the only "shadows of sound" surviving—the "drowsed cricket's chirp" or the mockingbird's "croon in sleep"—"But touch this sacred, soft tranquility/ To yet diviner quiet."

"The Inevitable Calm," on the other hand, offers a more generalized view of nature in a treatment of the truism "That after the Turmoil of Passion/ There cometh a time of rest." Written in the meter of Longfellow's "The Day is Done," it contains some of the most lyrical lines Hayne ever wrote, as the first two stanzas reveal:

> The sombre wings of the tempest,
> > In fetterless force unfurled,
> Buffet the face of beauty,
> > And scar the grace of the world.

> But they fade at length with the darkness,
> > And softly from sky to sod
> Peace falls like the dew of Eden,
> > From the opened palm of God.

A copy of this poem in manuscript was the occasion in 1878 for an exchange of remarks regarding regularity in rhythm or meter between Hayne and Mrs. Preston. Mrs. Preston urged him "to be careful never to change the two-syllabled word with which the 1st & 3rd lines of each stanza generally close, for a one-syllabled word." Hayne, who had done so only once, argued in reply in a letter of October 22 that some looseness might occasionally be necessary. To support his point, he cited Poe's discussion of Long-fellow's poem in *Marginalia* and concluded that this was a case where to be "correct would be inartistic," though he admitted: "Of course, the innovation of ending any line in poems of this bastard construction, by a monosyllable, is so very bold as to be perhaps *fantastic*. Still," he concluded, "I *occasionally* advocate even *that*." This statement, of course, is not to be adduced as evidence that Hayne was always ready to change accepted poetic standards; but it does suggest that he was not unwilling to depart from customary practice. Indeed, there are other instances in which he maintains that occasional irregularities are necessary to the creation of art.[5]

Nature is also the subject in "Hints of Spring" (*The Independent,* June 28, 1877), as the epigraph from Goethe clearly indicates; and the renewal of life motif that is common to such verse is intensified at the end by a personal plea from the sick poet. The first two stanzas are among Hayne's best in this vein and call to mind the great lines on this theme by Chaucer, Shelley, Browning, and others.

> A softening of the misty heaven,
> A subtle murmur in the air;
> The electric flash through coverts old
> Of many a shy wing, touched with gold;
> The stream's unmuffled voice, that calls,
> Now shrill and clear, now silvery low,
> As if a fairy flute did blow
> Above the sylvan waterfalls;
> Each mellowed sound, each quivering wing
> Heralds the happy-hearted Spring:
> Earth's best beloved is drawing near.
>
> Amid the deepest woodland dells,
> So late forlornly cold and drear,
> Wafts of mild fervor, procreant breaths
> Of gentle heat, unclose the sheaths
> Of fresh-formed buds on bower and tree;
> A spirit of soft revival looks
> Coyly from out the young-leaved nooks,
> Just dimpling into greenery;
> Through flashes of faint primrose bloom,
> Through delicate gleam and golden gloom,
> The wonder of the world draws near.

Two of the best of these nature lyrics pay tribute to the "winged poet" of the South, the mockingbird. "The First Mocking-Bird in Spring" (*The Independent,* May 18, 1876) is a short ode in three strophes in which a speaker muses on the immediate past whereabouts of the lately returned "sylvan troubadour" whose "boundless wealth" of "music free" has engaged the attention of his fellow creatures; indeed, "all Nature" hearkens to the "gush" of melody from the "laureate's" throat; but to man, the bird's song has meaning which transcends that of its momentary beauty. The poet-speaker wonders if some human spirit—some "Lesbian singer's" perhaps—has a "part" in "*our* nightingale" and "in some mystical, wild, undreamed-of way,/ Find [s] voice in thy bountiful strains today!"

In suggesting that the bird is something more than a mere bird, Hayne approaches the Romantic tradition of Shelley and Keats (particularly the latter); but in his second poem, "The Mocking-Bird. (At Night.)," he paints a picture which calls to mind the flight of Shelley's skylark. Called first "The Flying Singer" and published in *Lippincott's* for July, 1878, the lyric deserves to hold a high place in the canon of Hayne's work on Southern topics. On a "warm southern night" a "fairy shape of flame" flashed before the poet's eye as he pensively "strayed" down a lonely "forest dell."

> It rose in dazzling spirals overhead,
> Whence to wild sweetness wed,
> Poured marvellous melodies, silvery trill on trill;
> The very leaves grew still
> On the charmed trees to hearken; while for me,
> Heart-thrilled to ecstasy,
> I followed—followed the bright shape that flew,
> Still circling up the blue,
> Till as a fountain that has reached its height,
> Falls back in sprays of light
> Slowly dissolved, so that enrapturing lay,
> Divinely melts away
> Through tremulous spaces to a music-mist,
> Soon by the fitful breeze
>   How gently kissed
> Into remote and tender silences.

V *The Sonnets*

In this group of later poems Hayne has divided his work into two sections: "Sonnets. On Various Themes" and "Personal Sonnets." Despite such arbitrary classification, the first category includes a number of pieces which are also "personal." Indeed, the better sonnets are rather intensely personal. Thus in "Freshness of Poetic Perception" the poet-speaker watches year after year the "fadeless forests in their Titan grace," is "thrilled" by forest sounds and sights, and concludes that the "poet's mind is fresh as dew" and that his "clear child's soul finds something sweet and new" in every aspect of nature. This theme appears again in the Wordsworthian "Nature at Ease" in which nature is "rife/ With subtlest meanings":

> If, then, the reverent soul doth lean aright,
> Close to those voices of wood, wind, and wave,
> What wondrous secrets bless the spiritual ear,
> Born, as it were, of music winged with light,
> Sweeter than those strange songs which Orpheus gave
> To earth and heaven, while both grew dumb to hear!

And in "To the Querulous Poets" Hayne expresses his concern for nature by cudgeling "false" dreamers who set their "wail" to the "treble of our querulous time" and who "blight" the "sweet song of thrush, or nightingale."

Finally, "England," published in the *Youth's Companion* for February 26, 1880, expresses the longing for "ancestral shores" also stated in the longer lyric of the same title (see above, p. 112).

> But most I dream of Shropshire's meadow grass,
> Its grazing herds, and sweet hay-scented air;
> An ancient hall near a slow rivulet's mouth;
> A church vine-clad; a graveyard glooming south;
> These are the scenes through which I fain would pass;
> There lived my sires, whose sacred dust is there.

The second category of "Personal Sonnets" contains poems addressed to such well-known literary luminaries as Longfellow, Swinburne, and Carlyle, and to such lesser lights as George H. Boker, Edgar Fawcett, Jean Ingelow, and Margaret J. Preston—

all, save Carlyle, friends by correspondence. These sonnets are
actually tributes; the one to Boker, for example, praises the Pennsylvania poet as a sonneteer and reveals at the same time Hayne's
own joy in the form; but the first of two sonnets in honor of
Swinburne is perhaps the most successful of Hayne's efforts in
this vein:

> Not since proud Marlowe poured his potent song
> Through fadeless meadows to a marvellous main,
> Has England hearkened to so sweet a strain—
> So sweet as thine, and ah! so subtly strong!
> Whether sad love it mourns, or wreaks on wrong
> The rhythmic rage of measureless disdain,
> Dallies with joy, or swells in fiery pain,
> What ravished souls the entrancing notes prolong!
> At thy charmed breath pale histories blush once more:
> See! Rosamond's smile! drink love from Mary's eyes;
> Quail at the foul Medici's midnight frown.
> Or hark to black Bartholomew's anguished cries!
> Blent with far horns of Calydon wildly blown
> O'er the grim death-growl of the ensanguined boar! [6]

The themes of the sonnets are, therefore, not new; nor has
Hayne's technique changed materially except, perhaps, in terms
of degree in two instances. Though Hayne still prefers the Italian
form, he is not a slave to it; and, on occasion, he manages the sestet
in particular with freedom, especially in regard to rhyme scheme.
Moreover, the diction itself undergoes some modification. Words
such as "oft" and "fain" appear less frequently, as do archaisms
and other designedly poetic terms. The result is a language more
nearly akin to Wordsworthian notions, though assuredly one of
the lamp or study and not that of the street or field. In general,
the later sonnets seem in these ways more mature than the earlier
ones; the difference is not pronounced in some and is marked
in others chiefly by signs of a modest evolution; but the careful
reader will not fail to discern this development.

VI *Ballads*

Though several of Hayne's ballads were written for special
occasions and might readily be considered later with his occasional

poems, he put "Macdonald's Raid.—A.D. 1780," "The Battle of King's Mountain," "The Hanging of Black Cudjo," and "Charleston Retaken" in sequence and referred to them as his "Revolutionary Ballads." They all deal with the American Revolution in South Carolina; are motivated by an awareness of various centennial observances and by the desire to point out similarities existing between South Carolina's actions in the Revolutionary War and the Civil War; and, with the exception of "Charleston Retaken," are brought into being through the agency of a first-person narrator who participates in the stirring events depicted.

The first to appear, "Macdonald's Raid," came out in *Harper's Monthly* for July, 1876, an issue honoring the centennial of independence. Cast somewhat in the pattern of derring-do adopted by Simms in his romances, the ballad, like Simms's fiction, is based on sources—in this instance, Mason Locke Weems's life of Francis Marion and Hayne's own memories of tales he had heard as a "lad" from one of Marion's men (*Letters*, 376-77). Indeed, the ballad is narrated in such a fashion as to take on the air of a tale told by an old soldier to whatever circle of boys might be available to him. Sergeant Macdonald's raid on a strong British garrison is exciting enough for any audience, and Hayne's eight-line stanzas of dominantly anapestic couplets and the dramatic refrain of "down with the King!" capture convincingly the movement and action of the "escapade":

> We leaped up at his summons, all eager and bright,
> To our finger-tips thrilling to join him in fight;
> Yet he chose from our numbers *four* men and no more.
> "Stalwart brothers," quoth he, "you'll be strong as
>   fourscore,
> If you follow me fast wheresoever I lead,
> With keen sword and true pistol, stanch heart and
>   bold steed.
> Let the weapons be loaded, the bridle-bits ring,
> Then swift death to the Redcoats, and down with the King!"

The raid follows, the "foemen" show what "cowed spirits" they possess, and the patriot "brothers" dally for a moment with "friends" in the town; but, when the British finally gather their strength, Macdonald's little band "scampers" safely through enemy shot and shell to rejoin Marion's partisans. "*That* was a feat," the old soldier concludes; and he challenges the "fops" and "weaklings" of the present generation to swing sabers with him.

Such an account of the poem, of course, makes obvious its leanings toward melodrama and its romanticizing of war and tends to obscure its spirited rhetoric and its evocation of the esprit for which Marion's swamp fighters were well known. Hayne himself was aware that the "style" might be "too *antiquated*"— as he remarked somewhat defensively to Tyler in a letter of September 30, 1876—"to suit the present *fantastic taste,* which denies poetic merit to Macaulay's *'Lays'*; & sneers at Walter Scott's *Homeric* narratives in verse, as mere rhymed *novels* or *romances!*" (*Letters,* 356-57).

Hayne also applied this comment to "Charleston Retaken," despite marked differences between the two works in form and in technique. Published in *Appletons' Journal* two months after the first ballad, "Charleston Retaken" describes the departure of the British occupation forces in 1782 and the return of political and military authority to the patriots. Developed from the point of view of a contemporary Carolinian soldier, yet told in the first-person plural, the piece is cast (with two exceptions) in an eight-line, iambic stanza rhyming *abcbdefe*. As a poem, it is slower and more restrained in movement than "Macdonald's Raid," in keeping with a more deliberate action; and it is far less melodramatic, though drama is not lacking in the last march of the enemy and in the subsequent entry of the Continental troops who, having been greeted on every side by "tender-eyed" women, "hoary patriots," and "young girls" scattering flowers, carry on to "dog" the British "down to the harbor-mouth" from whence they put to sea in a fleet of "three hundred noble vessels":

> We strained our vision waveward,
>   Watching the white-winged ships,
> Till the vague clouds of distance
>   Wrapped them in half eclipse:
> And still we strained our vision
>   Till, dimmer and more dim,
> The rearmost sail, a phantom pale,
>   Died down the horizon's rim.

In form, rhyme scheme, and even content, "Charleston Retaken" recalls "Vicksburg," another ballad about a war-ravaged city; but

it is less intense in feeling than the earlier piece, and its development is less sharply focused. As a result, the reader has an impression of immediacy in the treatment of the bombardment of
Vicksburg which never materializes in the account of the freeing
of Charleston.

"The Hanging of Black Cudjo" and "The Battle of King's Mountain" are about events which transpired in 1780. They are also
alike in that each, written in quatrains of long lines rhyming *aabb*,
holds consistently to the view that Whigs are patriots and Tories
are not; and each is narrated in the first person by one who has
participated in the events he describes. Like "Macdonald's Raid,"
"Black Cudjo" is based upon "incidents" in Weems's life of Marion;
but, unlike all the other ballads and poems in the Complete Edition, it is in Negro dialect, a "quaint *patois*" which Hayne claims
in a prefatory statement to be an "*exact* representation of the
broken English spoken by the slaves" in the "low country of South
Carolina" during antebellum times. Narrated by a slave as loyal
as Marse Chan's Sam and almost as loquacious as Joel Chandler
Harris's Uncle Remus, the ballad recounts Cudjo's courage and
fidelity in a perilous time when the Tories, momentarily expecting
to capture his master, a local Whig leader, seek to exact information of "Mass Tom's" whereabouts from the Negro by hanging
him three times:

> Dey fling a tick rope rou' my neck, dey drawed
>   me quick and high,
> I seed a tousan' million star a-flashin' from de sky.
>
> And den I choke, and all de blood keep rushin'
>   to my head
> I tried to yell, but only groaned, and guggled low
>   enstead;
> Till ebbery ting growed black as nite, and my last
>   taut was, sho,
> Dis nigger is a gone coon now, he'll see de wuld
>   no mo'!

Despite the pain and the torture, Cudjo remains firm and refuses
to divulge his master's hiding place; and for his steadfastness and
loyalty "Mass Tom" offers to grant Cudjo his freedom and to give

him a house, land, and farming equipment. The slave's reply, like that of the faithful servant of Simms's Captain Porgy before him and of many loyal fictional "darkies" after him, is that he has everything he wants and that he wishes to stay with his master:

"I stays wid you, (sez I again,) I meck de
    nigger wuck,
I wuck myself, and may be, Boss, we'll bring
    back de ole luck:
But don't you pizen me no more wid talk ob
    "freedom sweet,"
But sabe dat gab to stuff de years of de next
    fool you meet!"

As Negro dialect verse, "The Hanging of Black Cudjo" is not inferior to most contemporaneous work by Irwin Russell, Sidney Lanier, or Thomas Nelson Page. Indeed, with the exception of "Christmas-Night in the Quarters," this poem holds its own as dialect and as characterization with the best that Russell, Lanier, and Page had to offer.[7] Written early in 1876, shortly after others had pioneered in the field, it nevertheless appeared soon enough to put Hayne in a good publishing position had he wanted it, but for two very plausible reasons he was not interested. There was little demand for such verse (the market was just beginning to open for dialect fiction—as Cable, Harris, Miss Murfree, and others were discovering); and, more importantly, Hayne as a serious poet viewed such efforts as "Black Cudjo" as "mere *curiosities*," though he also thought the ballad valuable "philologically & dramatically."

But "The Battle of King's Mountain" was another matter. Commissioned by the King's Mountain Centennial to commemorate on October 7, 1880, one of the great engagements of the American Revolution, the poem was well received on the occasion and was brought to the attention of a national audience later in the month in the November issue of *Harper's Monthly*. Though Hayne was aware of the honor involved, his health permitted him neither to read his "ode" in person nor even to appear at the celebration on the day in question. His friend and kinsman, Charles Colcock Jones, Jr., an Augusta lawyer and historian, served in his stead.[8]

Narrated in the first person by an "aged volunteer" on the fiftieth anniversary of the battle, the ballad actually is a rather partisan account of the fighting, spiced with the veteran's opinions regarding right and wrong, war, and faith. Near the beginning, for example, he offers reasons for his "heroic rage" as he rides to the conflict on "Rhoderic's bounding back":

> There are some wrongs so blackly base, the tiger
>   strain that runs,
> And sometimes maddens thro' the veins, of Adam's
>   fallen sons,
> Must mount and mount to furious height, which
>   only blood can quell,
> Who smite with hellish hate must look for hate
>   as hot from hell! [9]

His view of war follows immediately:

> And hide it as we may with words, its awful need
>   confessed,
> War is a death's-head thinly veiled, even warfare
>   at its best;
> But *we*—heaven help us!—strove with those by lust
>   and greed accurst,
> And learned what untold horrors wait on warfare
>   at its worst.

But those who die for a sacred cause, he maintains, are rewarded. In a dreamlike state after the day has been won, the old soldier hears the "voices" of "heroes who fought for right and law" and learns that his "friends who strove the battle tide to stem" have passed up "beyond the stars." Anticipating a skeptical response to this "high strain" from his audience, the speaker indirectly indicts modern doubt ("the roughest rider of my day shrank from the atheist's sneer") and concludes with an affirmation of faith:

> True faith goes hand in hand with power—faith
>   in a holier charm
> Than fires the subtlest mortal brain, the
>   mightiest mortal arm;
> And though 'tis right in stress of fight "to keep
>   one's power dry,"
> What strength to feel, beyond our steel, burns the
>   great Captain's eye!

In some ways, "King's Mountain," as Hayne first called it, is the best of these ballads. It is not so melodramatic as "Macdonald's Raid," yet it is more stirring than "Charleston Retaken" and more credible perhaps in its treatment of human nature than "The Hanging of Black Cudjo." It surely has its shortcomings, the chief of which is its preachy tone, though this characteristic in itself does not undermine the interpretation of the narrator's character. The view of the conflict as one between British wrong and colonial right is that expressed in the other ballads, an opinion which now seems as dated as the zealous patriotism described in them all.

These matters, however, did not seem so old-fashioned in 1880. Hayne, pleased with his work, wrote Jones on November 11, 1881, that he had "had room & opportunity . . . for *dramatic verve,* and vivid picturesque description." Jones thought that it had "the ring of immortality about it." Others were also generous. F. S. Saltus observed on November 1, 1880, that the poem was "an honor to American literature," and Edgar Fawcett wrote on November 19: "How lovely your ballad was in *Harper!* I don't think you have ever done finer work. Many of the lines are truly magnificent." Such praise again suggests the context of the literary world in which Hayne lived and had his being.

VII *Memorials and Occasional Verse*

Hayne included twelve poems under the general heading "In Memoriam" and four others under "Poems for Special Occasions." Yet these categories are quite arbitrarily chosen as one notes when reading the commemorative poem to Simms, which was written for a particular cause and occasion, and such pieces as "The Return of Peace" and the "Yorktown Centennial Lyric," neither of which is included in either classification; yet each was commissioned by an organization to celebrate a particular occasion.[10]

Of the memorial verse, the short pieces in honor of Longfellow, Taylor, and Lanier and the long poem in memory of Simms seem most worthy of mention. "Longfellow Dead," for example, is a tribute (a "marvellous requiem" and a "paean" too) to a "fair, mild-eyed king" who has reached "the spring-tide of the eternal years" to stand crowned "amid his peers,/ The grand immortals." Taylor is also visualized as taking his place with the immortals, in this case Shakespeare, Homer, Aristophanes, and Goethe. In

"To Bayard Taylor Beyond Us," his master, the great German poet, welcomes the newly arrived bard to the "liberal air of that wide heaven" in which the "earth's supremest souls" are manifested along the "paths of light."

The death of Lanier, however, leads Hayne to muse in "The Pole of Death" on the great mystery itself:

> The twilight deepens into night,—
>   That night of frozen breath,
> The rigor of whose Arctic blight,
>   We recognize as—death!
>
> But since beyond the polar ice
>   *May* shine bright baths of balm;
> Past its grim barriers' last device,
>   A crystal-hearted calm,—
>
> Thus, ice-bound Death that guards so well
>   His far-off, secret goal,
> May clasp a peace ineffable,
>   For some who reach his pole!
>
> My poet—is it thus with thee,
>   Beyond this twilight gray,—
> This frozen blight, this sombre sea,
>   Ah! hast thou found the Day? [11]

The monody on Simms was not only a tribute to an old friend but also an effort to support and promote the Simms Memorial Fund in Charleston. Written in 1877 when Hayne was in "exile" in Georgia and delivered "tolerably well" by Nathaniel Levin before a large audience at the Charleston Academy of Music on the night of December 13, the poem later appeared in pamphlet form and in Bryant's *Evening Post* for January 14, 1878.[12] A long, irregular ode in rhyme, "Simms" describes the powers of the old "Viking"—his imagination, fancy, and "bluff humor true"—and extols his devotion to the "shrine of home and country" and his example amidst adversity as the best a "noble people" had to offer. Such a man deserves homage

> Large as that splendid prodigality
> Of force and love, wherewith he stanchly wrought
> Out from the quarries of his own deep thought,
> Unnumbered shapes; whether of good or ill,

No puny puppets whose false action frets
On a false stage, like feeble *Marionettes;*
   But life-like, human still;
Types of a by-gone age of crime and lust;
Or, grand historic forms, in whom we view
   Re-vivified, and re-created stand,
The braves who strove through cloud-encompassed ways,
Infinite travail, and malign dispraise,
To guard, to save, to wrench from tyrant hordes,
By the pen's virtue, or the lordlier sword's
   Unravished Liberty,
The virgin huntress on a virgin strand!

Waxing eloquent, the speaker grows personal as, from his "exile's home," he recalls the past when he was a "joyful youth" and "stalwart-statured *Simms*" was in his "midmost" years. Simms's character and personality are conjured up, and his doughty spirit is viewed as triumphing over its foes on earth and as achieving immortality in heaven where, "like all true souls," it "dwells forever individualized," the "mortal creature's marvellous counterpart;/ Only exalted, nobler."

As a work of art, the monody leaves something to be desired: it is too long and rambling, too rhetorical and sentimental, too lacking in esthetic distance. Hayne himself was aware of some of its shortcomings, but the obvious affection for Simms is genuine, the criticism of his work is valid, the sketch of his character and personality is valuable, and the concluding section on immortality of the soul is a clear revelation of Hayne's own most cherished religious views.

There are only four occasional poems listed as such in the Complete Edition. These are tributes to Whittier, Oliver Wendell Holmes, Emerson, and Rowland G. Hazard, a Rhode Island friend and benefactor. Aside from the Simms monody, however, there are two other pieces—"The Return of Peace" and the "Yorktown Centennial Lyric"—which were written for special occasions, though they are not classified as such.

The lyrics addressed to Whittier and the others are all gracefully worded birthday greetings and were, with the exception of the last, requested by the Boston *Literary World* for separate issues honoring the three New England writers. The poem celebrating Hazard's birthday was called forth by Hayne's own grati-

tude for the wealthy Quaker's generosity and friendship.[13] The
concluding two stanzas of the compliment to Holmes may serve
as a representative sample of Hayne's contribution in this vein:

> Philanthropist! poet! romancer! combined—
> Ay! shrewd scientist too—who shall fathom your mind,
> Shall plumb that strange sea to the uttermost deep,
> With its vast under-tides, and its rhythmical sweep?
>
> You have toiled in life's noon, till the hot blasting light
> Blinds the eyes that would gauge your soul stature aright;
> But when eve comes at last, 't will be clear to mankind,
> By the length of bright shadow your soul leaves behind!

The two longer poems were both written in 1881 to be delivered
in October: "The Return of Peace" in Atlanta on the inauguration
of the International Cotton Exposition on October 5 and the
Yorktown poem at the Virginia shrine on the centenary of Corn-
wallis' surrender on October 19. Neither work adds much to Hayne's
stature as a poet, but it is significant in regard to his literary reputation that he (rather than another poet) commemorated these
occasions. If, indeed, Hayne as an adopted Georgian appeared
readily available to the authorities of the Atlanta "festival," the
Yorktown ceremonies, on the other hand, were national in character and scope, and Hayne was selected by the Yorktown Centennial Commission, a body created by Congress itself and composed
of members from throughout the country.[14]

"The Return of Peace" is another of Hayne's irregular rhymed
odes. With variations in scheme from couplets to long-delayed
rhyme, it recites Atlanta's anguish during the war ("a city ravished
and o'erthrown") and celebrates her "high-souled" courage in
shaking off the "lotus-languishment of grief" and in building "the
fresh foundations of a nobler sway" on the "ashes" of "war-wasted
lands." Thus the way was prepared for developments in industry
and commerce which have given her "bounteous empire" over
the South and led to the present "glorious festival." The last sections offer a vision of the future in which the poet-speaker sees
the city as no longer a "warrior-queen" but an "empress of all
peaceful ties," "all potent industries," and "all world-embracing
magnanimities." Famed in the world, Atlanta, he opines, will send

forth of its "opulent store" as "purveyor of divinest charity" and
as "love-commissioned almoner of God."

Not unlike the sentiments expressed near the end of "Ethnogenesis" and "The Cotton Boll" where Timrod prophesies a role
in world affairs for the Confederacy similar to that which Hayne
envisions in part for Atlanta, the ode did not please the Exposition
Committee, some members of which were concerned lest the
concentration on the city and the references to "the unfortunate
events of the war" should detract from the "international" character
of the festival. The committee's "judgment" was conveyed by
Hannibal I. Kimball, Director General of the Exposition, in a
letter of September 26, 1881. Pointing out that the committee's
view of the work differed from that which "directed" Hayne in
its preparation and also from his own "regard" for such "an appropriate and highly finished contribution," Kimball expressed
the desire of his colleagues "that the ode should not so prominently
identify the history, achievements and future of the city of Atlanta."
The committee, he concluded, especially desired "to have nothing
in the exercises predicated upon the unfortunate events of the war,
unless it be rejoicing over the erection here upon the abandoned
theater of war of all altars dedicated to peaceful and moral vic-
tories that shall add greater glories to the people and history of
our common country."

Since Kimball's only previous instruction had been that the
poem "be appropriate and serve to enhance the interesting character of the ceremonies and assist in making them memorable,"
Hayne, dismayed and disgruntled by the committee's action, refused to make any changes. When a somewhat embarrassed Kimball agreed with him and took the responsibility for having the ode
"read exactly as written," it was delivered by N. J. Hammond of
Georgia at the opening ceremonies on October 5 and published
in the *Constitution* on the next day. Hayne himself was not present
(the family was represented by Will), and there was little critical
response to the poem. To make matters worse, Hayne had difficulty
in collecting his fee ($100), which was not sent until December
19. He was, to put it mildly, chagrined and disillusioned by the
whole affair.[15]

The "Yorktown Centennial Lyric," on the other hand, is not
an ode but, as Hayne informed Mrs. Preston on June 20, 1881,
"a simple patriotic song in the anapestic measure . . . with a

sonorous rhythm & chorus calculated to be popular." Composed in five stanzas, it elaborates the cooperation between the colonials and the French in the defeat of the British, a theme which is epitomized with slight verbal variation in the last four lines, or "chorus," of each stanza save the fourth:

> Those banners united in love as in fame,
> The brave standard which drew from the star-beams
> their flame,
> And type of all chivalry, glory, romance,
> The lilies, the luminous lilies of France.

Stedman thought well of the poem. "It reads superbly in print," he wrote Hayne on October 21. "Nothing could have been finer, upon such an occasion, & the South has every right to be proud of her laureate," he added later. H. M. Alden and F. S. Saltus also praised the piece, but Hayne was not satisfied with it. It was, he remarked in the previously mentioned letter to Mrs. Preston, "in no *high* sense a poem"; "perhaps I should say, not a Poem at all; but a jingling series of stanzas, spirited enough (I hope), and true to the occasion, & its historical reminiscences." In November he wrote Jones that he would not "give" his King's Mountain ballad for "20" Yorktown lyrics. Months later he was still harping on the same theme to Jones: "I was hampered from the beginning," he lamented on March 15, 1882, "by the *strict requirements* of *technical music;* all opportunities . . . of dramatic treatment; and broad imaginative sequence & suggestion were thus denied me; hence the result: a *mere* Popular or Patriotic song, *pur et simple!*" This view is perhaps too harsh. The poem does possess a stately measure, is far more objective in tone and purpose than most of Hayne's efforts in this line, and, gauged strictly as an occasional piece, is better than Hayne supposed. But it nevertheless falls considerably short of Emerson's "Concord Hymn" and Timrod's Magnolia Cemetery "Ode," both of which were also written to be sung on special occasions.

VIII *Meditative and Religious Verse*

During the last five or six years of his life Hayne became increasingly interested in religion, an involvement which led him to write a number of poems on it and related topics. Some of the

best of these appear in this category in the Complete Edition:
"Consummatum Est," "The True Heaven," "A Little While I Fain
Would Linger Yet," "Twilight Monologue," "The Shadow of
Death," and "In Harbor." [16] Relatively brief lyrics though they
are, they deserve consideration not only for their poetic merit
but for the light they throw on Hayne's own views and faith.

All these poems express an awareness that life is drawing to
a close and that death is in the offing. With the possible exception
of "Consummatum Est," each, in one way or another, is a response
to the "shadow of death." "Consummatum Est" welcomes the
"sacred sleep" of "death's majestic quiet"; but it is primarily a
tirade against life's "false hopes," "futile ends," and "vain myths"
which merely serve to mock men. Only love, the speaker asserts,
"sanctifies the ruin" of man's dreams and "brave aims."

> I've done with all beneath the stars,
>   O world! so wanly fleeting!
> How long against time's ruthless bars
>   Have the soul's wings been beating,
> Till even the soul but yearns for sleep,
>   Calm rest for fevered riot—
> The sacred sleep, the shadows deep,
>   Of death's majestic quiet!

"The True Heaven," composed during the same period, suggests
that death may lead to a "marvellous state" of peace and action.
"True 'rest' or 'peace,'" Hayne assured Lipscomb on February
29, 1884, "is not 'quietism'"; and he urged him to read this poem
for what he felt to be the "correct" view of heaven. The "bliss"
men long for is in

> A heaven of action freed from strife,
>   With ampler ether for the scope
> Of an immeasurable life
>   And an unbaffled, boundless hope.
>
> A heaven wherein all discords cease,
>   Self-torment, doubt, distress, turmoil,
> The core of whose majestic peace
>   *Is godlike power of tireless toil.*

The other poems accept the inevitable with only a mild reluctance which usually manifests itself in a last request of life. The
lovely and often anthologized "A Little While I Fain Would
Linger Yet," another of his lyrics addressed to his wife, is the
yearning of one who knows his "life is almost set" but who "fain
would linger" for "love's sake";

> A little while, when night and twilight meet;
>   Behind, our broken years; before, the deep
>   Weird wonder of the last unfathomed sleep.
> A little while I still would clasp thee, Sweet;
> A little while, when night and twilight meet.
>
> A little while I fain would linger here;
>   Behold! who knows what soul-dividing bars
>   Earth's faithful loves may part in other stars?
> Nor can love deem the face of death is fair:
> A little while I still would linger here.

In a "Twilight Monologue" the request for time is equally heartfelt, though the object is not love but art. "As the twilight comes
down," the poet wonders if he has "lived, dreamed, and labored
in vain," and in anguish he cries out:

> O! thou genius of art! I have worshipped and
>   blessed;
>   O! thou soul of all beauty and light!
> Lift me up in thine arms, give me warmth from
>   thy breast,
>   Ere the twilight be merged in the night!
>
> Let me draw from thy bosom miraculous breath,
>   And for once, on song's uppermost height,
> I may chant to the nations such music in death
>   As shall mock at the twilight and night!

"The Shadow of Death," on the other hand, summarizes succinctly and memorably Hayne's feeling for nature and its meaning
in relation to the mystery of death. Composed in three seven-line
stanzas rhyming *abaabcc*, its attitude of entreaty is emphasized
by a petition in each stanza in which the speaker, under the
shadow of death, prays, in turn, to hear "the pine-trees'/ slum-

berous sighs," to lie "close to nature's pulses deep," and to cling
to "some fair shreds" of "earth's delight" as his spirit wings its
"upward flight":

> I pray you, when the shadow of death comes down,
> Oh! lay me close to nature's pulses deep,
> Whether her breast with autumn tints be brown,
> Or bright with summer, or hale winter's crown
> Press on her brows in sleep;
> So nigh the dawn of some new, marvellous birth,
> I'd look to heaven, still clasped in arms of earth!

Finally, "In Harbor," in the manner of Emerson's "Terminus"
and other poems foreshadowing the end of a career or death, fore-
sees a limit to the poet's life and work, though Hayne, like Emerson, lived for years after the publication of his piece. Hayne
described his purpose in a letter of July 3, 1882, to Nathaniel R.
Middleton, a former president of the College of Charleston: "*Subjective* in *one* sense, I yet strove to make the central idea *un-
egotistical*, sufficiently so, at all events, to embody (however
partially) the feeling of suffering Humanity worn & wasted by
long conflict,—but with the goal in view *at last!!*" (*Letters*, 203).
Designated to conclude "Later Poems," "In Harbor" is actually
followed by six poems; but there is no doubt that he intended it
to be his valedictory:

> I think it is over, over,
>   I think it is over at last,
> Voices of foeman and lover,
> The sweet and the bitter have passed:—
> Life, like a tempest of ocean
> Hath outblown its ultimate blast;
> There's but a faint sobbing sea-ward
> While the calm of the tide deepens lee-ward,
> And behold! like the welcoming quiver
> Of heart-pulses throbbed thro' the river,
>   Those lights in the harbor at last,
>   The heavenly harbor at last!
>
> . . . .
>
> I *know* it is over, over,
>   I know it is over at last!

> Down sail! the sheathed anchor uncover,
> For the stress of the voyage has passed:
> Life, like a tempest of ocean
>   Hath outbreathed its ultimate blast:
> There's but a faint sobbing sea-ward,
> While the calm of the tide deepens lee-ward;
> And behold! like the welcoming quiver
> Of heart-pulses throbbed thro' the river,
> Those lights in the harbor at last,
> The heavenly harbor at last!

IX *Laureate Poems*

Hayne, of course, did not include "Laureate Poems" as a heading in the Complete Edition, but it is the best way to characterize those poems written by him as the poetic spokesman for the South—a posture he assumed sometimes by request and sometimes on his own initiative on a number of public and political occasions. No effort is made to include all such poems nor to discuss all those so classified. Of the pieces not collected before this edition, the following are considered laureate statements: "To Alexander H. Stephens," "South Carolina to the States of the North," "The Stricken South to the North," "A Plea for the Gray," "Union of Blue and Gray," "The King of the Plow," "On the Death of President Garfield," "Hiram H. Benner," "The Death of Hood," and "Reconciliation," to take them in the order in which they appear.[17]

Two themes are dominant in these poems—the South in defeat and the reconciliation of the sections. Thus the sonnet to Stephens, the "Plea for the Gray," and "The Death of Hood" celebrate the resources of the region even in defeat—its statesmen, its soldiers, and its people;[18] and "South Carolina to the States of the North" protests Reconstruction practices, particularly those in South Carolina. The other poems elucidate in various ways the theme of reconciliation.

The most successful of these pieces—"South Carolina to the States of the North" and "The Stricken South to the North"— embody clearly Hayne's views on the two chief topics. The first, written in "heart's blood" shortly after the disputed Presidential election of 1876 and published a few weeks later in Augusta and Charleston newspapers, is addressed in the subtitle "especially to those that formed a part of the original thirteen" and is dedicated

to Wade Hampton, who eventully became governor of South
Carolina after the disputed election in the state was settled. Coming from the "very depths" of the poet's soul, the lyric rehearses
the "awful burden" of the "wrongs" done his state:

> I lift these hands with iron fetters banded:
>   Beneath the scornful sunlight and cold stars
> I rear my once imperial forehead branded
>   By alien shame's immedicable scars;
> Like some pale captive, shunned by all the nations,
>   I crouch unpitied, quivering and apart—
> Laden with countless woes and desolations,
>   The life-blood freezing round a broken heart!

"Northmen," South Carolina claims, have "torn" "Freedom" from
her "side"; and, when the reply comes that it is a *"tyrant-party's*
treacherous action" and not the North's responsibility, the spirit
of the state recalls its "ancient glory"; vows to take action; and,
vanquishing its "foes" and upholding its "laws," smites *"Wrong"*
with the *"ballot,"* only to find the "tyrant's sword" again "glittering" at its "throat" and its "chains" reunited:

> There towers a judgment-seat beyond our seeing;
>   There lives a Judge, whom none can bribe or blind;
> Before whose dread decree, your spirit fleeing,
>   May reap the whirlwind, having sown the wind:
> I, in that day of justice, fierce and torrid,
>   When blood—*your* blood—outpours like poisoned wine,
> *Pointing to these chained limbs, this blasted forehead,*
>   *May mock your ruin, as ye mocked at mine!*

The response to the poem, even from Northerners, was generous.
Edgar Fawcett wrote Hayne on March 26, 1877, that it was a
"very noble & lovely piece of work . . . altogether . . . majestic,
sonorous, and of striking lyrical beauty," though he normally considered political topics ephemeral and not appropriate for poetry.
"Still," he concluded, "I congratulate you heartily upon its rhythmical stateliness, and cannot but feel, after all, that you must hold
it a piece of pen-service by no means thrown away upon the distressing complexities which have called it forth." Holmes, two weeks
later on April 11, praised the "eloquence and force" of the lyric

and observed: "I could not call up the images which your poem pictured in words the intensity of which showed how deep the feeling which prompted them without a thrill of sympathy and an aching of regret that my fellow countrymen of your proud record and sensitive race should be doomed to such suffering." [19] T. B. Aldrich sounded a similar note on April 26. After assuring Hayne that he had "done nothing stronger or finer than some of the stanzas in 'South Carolina to the States of the North,'" Aldrich remarked: "There is not an honest man this side of Mason & Dixon's line who is not indignant at the way the South has been treated. . . . I hope," he concluded, "a new day has dawned for our whole country, and here's to the confusion of all political knaves, North and South!"

Whatever may be said of the poem now, it remains Hayne's most intense and passionate lyric on a political subject. Despite its dated diction and images and its declamatory style, it still goes, as Jay B. Hubbell pointed out in *The South in American Literature*, "straight to the mark" and "is not wanting in strength" (756).

"The Stricken South to the North" takes up the reconciliation theme and pays tribute to those who sought to alleviate the suffering caused by the yellow-fever epidemics of 1878. Printed in the place of honor on the editorial page of the New York *Sun* on October 6 and dedicated to Holmes, an active contributor to drives in behalf of the victims, the poem pictures the South just emerging from the aftermath of war to "rhythms of healthful joy and brave desire" when a "doom that blasts the blood and blights the breath" falls upon it. At that moment, a "voice of manful cheer and heavenly trust" is heard, and a "hand redeeming"

> Rolls back the curtain of malignant darkness,
>   And shows the eternal blue of heaven again—
> Revealing there, o'er worlds convulsed and shaken,
>   That face whose mystic tenderness enticed
> To hope new-born earth's lost bereaved, forsaken!
>   Ah! still beyond the tempest smiles the Christ!
>
> Whose voice? Whose hand? Oh, thanks, divinest Master,
>   Thanks for those grand emotions which impart
> Grace to the North to feel the South's disaster,
>   The South to bow with touched and cordial heart!

> Now, now at last the links which war had broken
>   Are welded fast, at mercy's charmed commands;
> Now, now at last the magic words are spoken
>   Which blend in one two long-divided lands!
> O North! you came with warrior strife and clangor;
>   You left our South one gory burial ground;
> But love, more potent than your haughtiest anger,
>   Subdues the souls which hate could only wound!

Such a gesture, of course, could not help appealing to many in the North. Holmes wrote on October 16 thanking Hayne "very cordially" for the "eloquent and feeling lines" and for the "compliment" of the dedication. Then he added: "I am thankful at least that out of this unutterable woe should have grown some healing influences." Whittier sent his opinion of "that noble poem" a month later. "My whole heart responds" to it, he acknowledged on November 12 and then continued: "God knows that our people felt only that you needed aid; & that you were our fellow countrymen. The sad past was thrown so far back that it was not remembered." And early in the new year, John Welsh, United States Minister to the Court of Saint James, caused the poem to be reprinted in the *Anglo-American Times* for January 24, 1879, and expressed his congratulations in a letter of the same date.

Though Hayne was paid only ten dollars for the poem, the circulation and national publicity attendant on its appearance in the *Sun* and the subsequent publication in the same paper five weeks later of "Hiram H. Benner," a poem memorializing the unselfish efforts and later martyrdom of a courageous army officer, a former Union soldier, to carry relief supplies into the yellow-fever country south of Saint Louis, led many to associate Hayne with the cause of reconciliation, a view he did not hesitate to promote, especially among his Northern friends and correspondents.

X *Critical Reaction*

The Complete Edition was slow in making its way to the critics and the public, for Lothrop was chary of sending out review copies, and Hayne apparently received no royalty payments prior to his death; still, the book had an impact on those who read it.[20] Mrs. Preston, for example, noted on December 11, 1882, that it was a "rich collection." Others soon joined her in complimenting the poet. Mrs. M. B. M. Toland, an old friend and amateur poet herself, wrote effusively on January 9, 1883: "Yours are the *best American poems* I ever read. They should wear our country's laurel wreath." On March 3 Hamilton Wright Mabie, a member of the *Christian Union* staff, characterized the volume as being "full of the bouquet of genuine poetry." Not long afterward on April 7 Philip Bourke Marston, the blind British poet and a friendly correspondent, praised Hayne's imagination for its flexibility in passing from "grave to gay, from the sternnesses of philosophy to the fragrant delicacies of love." And two years later on February 7, 1884, Mrs. Julia Dorr admitted that, familiar as she was with his verse, she "was not prepared for the wealth and poetic splendor of the volume."

The chief accolade, however, had come earlier from E. C. Stedman, who was to Hayne and many others of the day "the greatest of American Art-Critics." In a letter of December 20, 1882, a "communication" which Hayne put "straightway" among his "most cherished epistolary archives," Stedman acknowledged Hayne's letter of December 10 with its "portentous list of *errata*" to the Complete Edition. "Luckily they cannot blight the rich fruitage of your Muse. We all know the successive vintages you have given us, and are glad to have them blended in this brimming and generous vat. On the whole, your 'Complete Edition' is a beautiful success—in every way such a voucher & witness as an American poet may be proud to bring forward. There is something in dimensions, as Landor has asserted, & one now sees, for the first time, how important and genuine your life-long [*sic*] has been. Nor is there,' he concluded, "an affected, careless, untrue piece of workmanship in the entire collection."

The reviewers were also frequently generous in their treatment of the book, but there is naturally less agreement among the critics than among Hayne's correspondents. Maurice Thompson, for example, in a review in the Indianapolis *Times* for March 4, 1883, notes Hayne's limitations due to "sectional bias" yet considers his latest work his best and ranks him as one of the four "best known" living poets of America. "It is not saying too much," Thompson asserts, "that in this volume . . . is shut some of the best verse, of the worthiest and wholesomest kind, that has been made in this country."

Charles Deshler in *Harper's Monthly* for June, 1885, sounds more judicious to modern ears. He praises the "maturer poems" for their "melody" and "impassioned poetic feeling" and for their pictures of nature's "changeful and glowing features," but he is not unaware of faults and weaknesses. "Many of the poems," he observes, "are immature, many are defective in some detail of form or spirit, but in all there is visible a sensitive and loyal conscientiousness begotten of their author's ever-present idea of the loftiness and dignity of the poet's calling, with the effect of curbing the vagaries of his rich and versatile fancy and chastening his active imagination."

A writer in the *Literary World* for March 19, 1883, comes even closer to the twentieth-century view of Hayne's stature. He likes the nature poems well enough, though he sees them as considerations of the "external aspects of nature"; and, unlike Mrs. Preston, he decides that they do not measure up to Wordsworth's; and he concludes that Hayne is entitled to an "honourable place among the minor American poets." The critical spectrum, then, was broad and generally fair, representing judgments which were justified in the nineteenth century but which have stood less well the test of time.

CHAPTER 6

"Last Poems," 1882-1886

SHORTLY after the Complete Edition came out in the fall of 1882 Hayne began making plans for a second edition which would correct errors, add new poems, and sell for a cheaper price. But this was not to be, for despite the acknowledgment of publisher and editor regarding the book's faults, they were not convinced that these justified such a venture when, at the same time, the sale was so "limited." Consequently, the best poems of the last four years of Hayne's career were not collected during his life, and since, after his death, the Lothrop firm, in effect, thwarted the efforts of his widow and his son to bring out a new edition or to collect the late verse, these poems have remained uncollected and unanthologized to the present time. In discussing them (many for the first time), I follow generally the arrangement made by Will Hayne for the proposed volume he called "The Last Poems of Paul Hamilton Hayne": prelude, poems for public occasions, memorial poems, miscellaneous poems, sonnets, and quatrains.[1]

The prelude is, appropriately enough, "Face to Face," a valedictory piece and one of Hayne's best poems on any topic. Published in *Harper's Monthly* for May, 1886, a few weeks before his final illness, the poem was first called "The Seer on Death," a title which Mrs. Hayne later suggested be changed to "Face to Face." The view of death expressed in the piece, hardly new with Hayne, had been anticipated earlier in his verse, especially in "At Last," a sonnet printed in *Harper's Bazar* in 1874 in which death is pictured as a "pale phantasmal shade" whose "mask" at life's last "mortal breath" melts away like a "nightmare dream" and reveals instead, "smiling," "heaven's high-priest of Immortality!" "Face to Face" offers the same idea but more confidently and at greater length. In Poesque manner and meter, a seer seeks in the first stanza to assure man that death is not what he supposes but that its "unveiled face" reveals the "glory of love." Three succeeding stanzas continue the argument the speaker has urged, and the last four lines of each, a refrain in very slightly varied form, repeat the notion that death is love. The point is clinched in the fifth and final stanza:

> But beyond the stars and the sun
>   I can follow him still on his way,
> Till the pearl-white gates are won
>   In the calm of the central day.
> Far voices of fond acclaim
>   Thrill down from the place of souls,
> As Death, with a touch like flame,
>   Uncloses the goal of goals;
> And from heaven of heavens above
>   God speaketh with bateless breath—
> My angel of perfect love
>   Is the angel men call Death!

The idea is simple and accurately reflects Hayne's faith at the time. What it lacks in philosophical or theological profundity it makes up for in sincerity and serenity, and when the poem is viewed in the context of Hayne's life, its expression of tranquil acceptance becomes all the more poignant and meaningful. "Face to Face," assuredly, contains some of the weaknesses of a conventional Romanticism evident in the poet's earlier work, but as a valedictory it shares a place of honor with "In Harbor" and is not unworthy of being mentioned in the same breath with similar contemporaneous pieces, such as Emerson's "Terminus" and Browning's "Prospice" and "Epilogue" to *Asolando*.

I *"Sesqui-Centennial Ode"*

On December 20, 1882, William Bogart, a member of the committee in charge of arrangements for the Savannah Sesquicentennial, wrote Hayne requesting a poem for the occasion. He declined at first because of the delicate state of his health; but when Henry Rootes Jackson, president of the committee and a prominent Georgian, and Charles Colcock Jones, Jr. both urged him to reconsider, Hayne relented and agreed to write an ode.

Taking a few hints from Jones's pamphlet *Historical Sketch of Tomo-chi-chi, Mico of the Yamacraws* (1868) and warming to his work, he completed the poem in time for the public reading on February 12, 1883, and for publication the next day in the Savannah *Morning News* and the Atlanta *Constitution.*

An irregular ode of 325 lines usually paired in couplets with occasional variations in delayed rhyme, the poem commemorates the establishment of the Georgia colony; celebrates the parts played by "majestic and immortal" Oglethorpe, the founder, and by Tomo-chi-chi, the "Western forest's noblest denizen"; compliments Savannah for its contributions to the past and present; visualizes Georgia's future; and apostrophizes the state as the poet's "Second Mother."

Generally in the old-fashioned rhetorical style of verse meant for public declamation, the ode is an eloquent tribute to Oglethorpe and, in particular, to Georgia, the apostrophe to which at the end makes a fitting climax to the poem and the occasion. Recognizing his debt to his adopted home which gave him "bread and balm and wine" when his "Mother-Land," South Carolina, was "struck down by hands of aliens," "robbed by the hireling Hound," and "scourged by the Boor and throttled by the Slave," the poet speaks in his own voice and pours out his heart in gratitude to Georgia for offering a beneficent nature to write about and for bringing peace to his soul. Wishing to "exalt" the state's "loveliness," he finds that his "measure falters" and his "numbers fail":

> Thus, brave Protectress! at thy shining feet,
> Alas! alas! 'tis only mine to lay
> This simple wild-flower wreath of votive song!
> I know (how well) it does thy greatness wrong:—
> Still, oh Beloved! wilt Thou lift it now,
> One moment to thy white, imperial brow?
> And if some glittering moisture here and there,
> The bay-leaf and the blossom chance to wear,—
> Pluck not the garland from thy stately head;—
> 'Tis but a few glad tears thy Poet shed,
> To keep his grateful offering pure and sweet!

The unabashed Romantic posture and the elaborate diction represent aspects of style which render the poem somewhat passé now. Even its sincerity and genuine passion contribute to its dated qualities, and though (as Lipscomb observed in 1885) the ode "embodies" and "signalizes" Hayne's character, culture, and gifts, this too suggests a tradition whose nature and resources by the late nineteenth century have become largely derivative and lacking in native sustenance.

Nevertheless, the poem was well received in Savannah (the poet and his family had attended the celebration, though he had not been able because of a "throat-affection" to recite his work), a "great success" Hayne wrote Mrs. Preston on February 27. "Why," he added, "they could not have paid me greater honor, had I been Tennyson (!!)" The sesquicentennial committee responded handsomely by awarding him $500 for his "performance," and Georgians generally praised it. Chancellor Lipscomb, for example, called it "the most admirable ode ever produced in the South." Other criticism was also favorable, especially after the poem was published as a pamphlet in 1885. Moses Coit Tyler wrote on January 26, 1886, of his admiration for its power and beauty, and Hamilton Wright Mabie commented in the *Christian Union* on its "genuine poetic feeling" and concluded that "nothing stronger had been written in the South for many a day." That "day" has come and gone, and the "Sesqui-Centennial Ode" now is of importance chiefly as a late manifestation of Hayne's muse. But, dated though it is, it remains an interesting example of an occasional poem that is also very personal and that reveals as much about the poet as it does about the occasion.

II *Smith College Poem*

In the late summer of 1882 Margaretta M. Osgood, a senior at Smith College and chairman of a student committee, wrote Hayne that he had been nominated by the students to compose a poem for delivery at the graduation exercises of the class of 1883. Pleading his "uncertain health," the poet was allowed to delay the final decision until January, at which time he agreed to undertake the commission. The poem was ready in May, read at commencement on June 22 by J. Wesley Churchill of Andover Theological Seminary, and printed first in Northampton's *Hampshire County Journal* on June 23 and thereafter in pamphlet form as "A Poem Written for the Graduating Class of 1883, Smith College."

A long, irregular lyric divided into fifteen sections, the piece offers the poet-speaker an opportunity to express in an oracular fashion his views on women and on religion; and, for one whose earlier opinions on the former had been rather old-fashioned and on the latter somewhat unorthodox and erratic, the Smith College poem is an important statement of his latest thoughts on the two topics.

From beautiful"Georgian hills"the poet's spirit, a "gleeful Ariel," "blithely navigates" a cloud shaped like an "elemental Argo" to "quaint Northampton Town" where it joins the "fair" graduates on the "festal day." Reviewing quickly the progress made by women over the ages, the speaker happily notes that "old errors" have died and that "old forms" have declined in this "nobler age of ours." The "chains of custom" have been "loosened," and woman is now free to examine intellectually the wonders of science and art, but her doing so does not mean at all that she is to "assert equality with man," forget her place as wife or mother, or be misled by a "spirit of measureless pride" to "dark unfaith." Though the lot of mankind may be mortal ("all mortal trophies droop at last"), there is "comfort" in the all-sufficient "eternal love" represented by the "marvelous Nazarene," the "Man-God that mak'st the lep'rous clean":

> Ah me! whatever wisdom man may claim,
> Immaculate and immortal, finds its type
> Of trust unsullied and of peace supreme,
> In one grand figure, (long in soul translated),
> Of that "Last Supper" which Da Vinci painted
> With inspiration of a genius sainted,—
> *The loved Disciple on the heart of Christ!*

Such faith is characteristic of Hayne during his last years, and the attitude expressed toward woman's *"true"* mission," while hardly radical in thrust, is nevertheless more liberal than that of many of his contemporaries and surely not entirely consonant with the usual view of Hayne as an arch-reactionary in all things social or political.

The lyric itself is quieter in tone and more temperate in purpose than are the occasional pieces on other topics more personally engaging to Hayne. There is evidence of a growing assurance in the handling of the particular verse form. The sections are usually verse paragraphs or statements complete in themselves though related to each other by the progression of thought. The rhyme scheme follows the stanzaic pattern and continues earlier experiments in delayed rhyme. Four of the lines quoted above, for example, end with words which occur so far in advance as to leave the ear unaware of the rhyme. No line is left dangling without an eventual mate, but neither sight nor sound is cloyed with uninterrupted rhyme, as is the case in much of Lanier's poetry or in Hayne's own earlier verse. Altogether, the Smith College poem shows that the poet has not stopped growing in thought or in technique.

III *Charleston Centennial Poem*

Written shortly after the effort in behalf of the Smith students at the request of his old friend, W. A. Courtenay, mayor of Charleston, "Poem upon the One Hundredth Anniversary of the Incorporation of the City of Charleston, S.C." is different in tone and form from the earlier piece. A tribute to a "stainless Maid of ocean," the city of his "Fathers' love," the lyric is an outburst of patriotism and nostalgia and also a farewell to his old home. The theme, as he wrote Mrs. Preston on August 23, 1883, is the "constancy and martyr-like courage of my native city by the sea." A highly personal poem, the balladlike quatrains (the long lines notwithstanding) suggest movement and appropriately reflect and enhance the strong feelings expressed.

Beginning with Revolutionary times, the poet celebrates the city's history, its part in three wars, its courage in defeat in the Civil War, its return to autonomy under Wade Hampton at the end of Reconstruction, and its achievement ("A golden Day *has* dawned at last!") under Courtenay's leadership. The last stanzas (XVI-XVII) form an apostrophe to the "land of lost content" where the poet cannot come again:

> Quaint City of my youth, farewell! no more
>   these eyes may quiver,
> Dazed by the glint of surf and sail on
>   flickering bar or river,
> No more these weary limbs may own the soul's
>   imperious order,

> To bear me where the sun-caps flash beyond
>   thy billowy border!
>
> Brave City of my youth, farewell! . . . When
>   safe from midday riot
> Kissed by the slumberous star that sways
>   her lotus-land of quiet,
> I still shall see thro' half-closed lids thy
>   moonlight beauty beaming,
>
> And hear St. Michael's mellowed bells swoon
>   down the tides of dreaming!

Read by his brother-in-law Dr. Middleton Michel at the ceremonies on August 14 and printed in the Charleston newspapers, the poem was well received by several of Hayne's fellow poets. G. Herbert Sass, also a Charlestonian, wrote that it was "worthy both of the subject and of your reputation"; and Henry Lyndon Flash, a minor Louisiana bard, termed the lyric "one of the very best you have written." The Charleston City Council expressed its appreciation by passing appropriate resolutions and by ordering a gold medal "suitably mounted and inscribed" for the laureate of the occasion. Touched and honored, Hayne acknowledged this recognition on October 15; he never heard Saint Michael's "mellowed bells" again.

IV *"The Broken Battalions"*

The occasion for which "The Broken Battalions" was composed was perhaps less auspicious than those which prompted the odes to anniversary celebrations at Savannah and Charleston, but Hayne was moved by the cause and by the times to write one of his most eloquent lyrics in behalf of a fund for the relief of Confederate veterans in Baltimore in 1885. Mrs. Hetty Cary Martin, who with her sister Jennie had set the words of James Ryder Randall's "Maryland, My Maryland" to the music of "Tannenbaum, O Tannenbaum," requested a contribution from Hayne in a letter of March 13; and, responding with alacrity, he wrote "The Broken Battalions" for the charity bazaar. The theme appealed to him powerfully ("my heart was full, and my brain aflame"), as he informed Lipscomb on March 27. In an exalted mood, he put on March 30 the finishing touches to the poem, which is at once a tribute to the Confederate dead, a plea for a proper honoring of the past, and a stoic acceptance of the outcome of the struggle lost twenty years earlier. Addressed, in effect, to his "Brothers," a speaker in the lyric delivers it as something of an exhortation to them to forgive, accept, and yet remember:

> The sounds of the tumult have ceased to ring,
>   And the Battle's Sun has set,
> And here in peace of the new-born Spring,
>   We would fain forgive and forget;
>
> . . . .
>
> We may scourge from the Spirit all thought of ill
>   In the midnight of grief held fast,
> And yet, O Brothers! be loyal still
>   To the sacred and stainless Past!

There is "duty still to be done" to the past, to the dead heroes:

> O, God! they come not as once they came
>   In the magical years of yore;
> For the trenchant sword and the soul of flame,
>   Shall quiver and flash no more;—

The "broken and battered hosts" are gone, those who fought with Lee and Jackson are no more; but they rate a salute as men who were not "vanquished" but "crushed by a mystic fate," and who will be remembered in the hearts of a grateful people:

> No Palace is here for the heroes' needs,
>   With its shining portals apart;—
> Shall they find the peace of their "Invalides,"
>   O, South! in your grateful—Heart?
>
> A Refuge of welcome with living halls,
>   And Love for its radiant dome,
> 'Till the music of death's reveille calls
>   The souls of the Warriors—home!

Deep feeling is bodied forth and yet controlled by the sure hand of the craftsman. The sentiments are clear, and the style and form are managed to convey them to best effect. The iambic and anapestic lines suggest the right movement and provide a contrast, and the four-line stanza holds the expression of emotion within proper limits. "The Broken Battalions" may not be a perfect poem; it surely is not a great one; but it is the best Hayne ever wrote in behalf of the Confederate cause.

V *Memorial Poems*

Under "Memorial Poems" appear six poems memorializing Senator B. H. Hill, Alexander H. Stephens, Charles Reade, Victor Hugo, "Chinese" Gordon, and Gordon's "betrayer." [2] They are not among Hayne's best late verse, but they show that he kept up with current affairs; and they embody his opinions on matters literary and political. The poems on Reade and Hugo, for example, clearly reveal his preferences in fiction. "Charles Reade. In Memoriam" ends on this note:

> No fine anatomist wert thou! Thine art was hale
>   and stout;
> Thy women and thy men were not turned, deftly,
>   inside out;
> Nor didst thou deem, as some do now, that
>   Fiction's loftiest hope
> Lies in the skill wherewith we use the psychal
>   microscope!
>
> O! grand thine eloquence in life, to counsel,
>   warn, or save;
> But grander those carved words of power, which
>   sublimate thy grave.

"Victor Hugo" expresses Hayne's view that the late novelist is a "Titan sun," the greatest of all French writers:

> For, lover of high things, brave conqueror, he
>   Hath won for bride a beauty not less fair
>   Than *she* who wears the starshine in her hair
> And on her lips the morning kiss of God!
> Thou, Death! hast stretched a priestly hand abroad,
>
>   And softly sanctified in all men's sight
>   The unperturbed, immaculate spousal rite,
> Binding together through all years to be
> Such Genius and such Immortality!

On the other hand, the pieces devoted to Hill and Stephens honor two Georgia political leaders Hayne admired very much, and "Gordon" pays tribute to the "dauntless" hero of Khartoum, a compliment echoed in " 'Habet,' " a denunciation of "Gordon's betrayer" and "Khartum's foul traitor." Gordon is the type of "antique chivalry":

> 'Twas a Coeur de Leon's hand once more
>   Which the Lion flag led on;
> But the soul of the dauntless soldier bore
>   The chrism of pure St. John.

His "Judas" is scorned even by the elements: " '*Habet!*' '*he has it!*' the hot breezes say"; and, though the traitor is dead, the desert sun in the form of "one swift, sharp sunbeam," as "'twere a rapier blade unsheathed," seeks to plunge "insatiate" into his "throbless heart"; "And thus, beyond the spectre of a doubt,/ Let the last curdled drop of treachery out!"

Altogether, the memorial poems are disappointing. They are not mere verses made for bread nor penned to catch the public eye, for Hayne felt deeply about these men and the things they represented. But, despite Lipscomb's warm praise of the Hugo and Gordon pieces and the enthusiasm of Philip Bourke Marston and R. D. Blackmore for the Reade memorial, these poems appear in the light of a new day as rather topical and ephemeral, even in idea if not in purpose or ideal, as effective recognition of the honored dead at the time perhaps, but hardly as substantial and enduring works of art in their own right.

VI *Miscellaneous Poems*

Under "Miscellaneous Poems" Will Hayne placed a number of his father's lyrics on various subjects, two of which, nature and religion, are of paramount importance to any consideration of his last work. These poems on nature are substantial treatments of a favorite topic; and together with several others not included in the collection, they constitute a sustained attempt to deal with the "heart of humanity" in a traditional fashion but in a contemporary agricultural setting. Beginning in February, 1882, these pieces appeared in *Home and Farm,* a popular national journal headquar-

tered at Louisville and aimed at a rural audience; and they were
the result of an "arrangement" made with Hayne by R. W. Knott,
the editor, "for a number of poems illustrating the various aspects
of life on a farm." For three years thereafter he published frequently and regularly in the periodical and was well paid for his
work—so well in fact that, when he learned of *Home and Farm*'s
retrenchment in 1885, he wrote Will on March 9 that it was a
"serious matter."[3]

Six of these agricultural lyrics are included in this collection.[4]
The earliest, "In the Wheat Field," which appeared in the issue of
August 1, 1882, exhibits several characteristic Hayne touches. The
point of view, for instance, is that of a poet standing in the "pearly
wheat"; although he is reveling sensuously in the sights, sounds,
and smells, the ultimate experience elaborated in the poem is his
love for his wife. Using the rich diction of Spenser and Keats, he
sees, feels, and reports on a day in the fields of "whispering wheat"
from dawn to eve. At dawn he becomes aware of the "early breath
of the wakening rose" and of the "subtle odor of Southern seas"
brought by a "sportive breeze," and he observes the "flashing wings
of the swallows" sweep over the wheat. But

> Aurora faints in the fulgent fire
>   Of the Monarch of Morning's bright embrace,
> And the summer day climbs higher and higher
>   Up the cerulean space;
> The pearl-tints fade from the radiant grain,
>   And the sportive breeze of the ocean dies,
> And soon in the noontide's soundless rain
>   The field seems graced by a million eyes;
> Each grain with a glance from its lidded fold,
> As bright as a gnome's in his mine of gold,
> While the slumbrous glamour of beam and heat
> Glides over and under the windless wheat.

And so to noon, twilight, and evening:

> Yet the languid spirit of lazy Noon,
>   With its minor and Morphean music rife,
> Is pulsing in low, voluptuous tune
>   With summer's lust of life.

Hark! to the droning of drowsy wings,
　　To the honey-bees as they go and come,
To the "boomer," scarce rounding his sultry rings,
　　The gnat's small horn and the beetle's hum;
And hark to the locust!—Noon's *one* shrill song—
Like the tingling steel of an elfin gong,
Grows lower through quavers of long retreat
To swoon on the dazzled and distant wheat.

Now Day declines! and his shafts of might
　　Are sheathed in a quiver of opal haze;
Still thro' the chastened, but magic light,
　　What sunset grandeurs blaze!

. . . .

Thus Eve creeps slowly and shyly down
　　And the gurgling notes of the swallows cease,
They flicker aloft through the foliage brown,
　　In the ancient vesper peace;
But a step like the step of a conscious fawn
　　Is stealing—with many a pause—this way,
'Till the hand of my Love thro' mine is drawn,
　　Her heart on mine, in the tender ray;
O hand of the lily, O heart of truth,
O Love, thou art faithful and fond as Ruth;
But *I* am the gleaner—of kisses—Sweet,
While the starlight dawns on the dimpling wheat!

The melody of this poem frequently takes precedence over the meaning, and the note of romance at the end has not been adequately prepared for. Moreover, the language, too consciously poetic, hardly suggests the idiom of the field or farm; and the point of view is too subjective to serve as an effective means of technique or of achieving appropriate esthetic distance. Some of the same objections may be leveled against Lanier's "Corn" though his ode is generally a better poem than Hayne's. A significant flaw in both pieces is that each falls short of reality in failing, for example, to consider what it was like to hoe corn or glean wheat. Yet this criticism is primarily one based on twentieth-century standards. In the context of its tradition, of its place of publication, and of Hayne's other verse, "In the Wheat Field" appears more successful and a not unworthy addition to the poet's canon.

Some of these observations may be applied generally to the other farm lyrics, but each has its own quality. "Seed Visions," for example, is a long irregular odelike piece in couplets that features a series of "visions of the storied past" that are strung together by an unidentified speaker who uses the first-person plural chiefly and who rather confusingly relates the visions to each other in terms of thought—the common point being that all have to do with "seed-time and harvest," from the time of Ararat to that of Christ, from Semiramis to Helen of Troy and back to ancient Ceres herself. It has some good lines, especially those near the beginning which personify "Drouth," "that veiled assassin of the air" who wilts the grass and "saps the souls" of the "woodland's mightiest boles" with the "hot Hades born in him." The diction, furthermore, is less ornate than that of other agricultural pieces; but, as a whole, "Seed Visions" is less satisfying than "In the Wheat Field," for the sequence of its visions is not justified, nor is its idea fulfilled.

Three other poems treat various phases of planting and harvesting. "Harvest Time," written in September, 1882, is a paean of thanksgiving for "Plenty" and "Peace" and is notable for its tribute to cotton (prior to this time the big money crop of the South had with one or two exceptions seldom been mentioned in Hayne's poetry):

> through shadowy hollow,
> Gleams the white splendor of the *Plant of Peace,*
> Its bolls, wind-wafted on their airy stations,
> Hold spells of subtlest service, deftly furled—
> Soon to unfold through marvelous transformations
> And weave their warmth and comfort 'round the world!

"The Genius of Midsummer Lands," on the other hand, is less noteworthy as a treatment of "harvest homes to be"; but it does express Hayne's recurring concern about death, though the question about his future the poet-speaker poses to the "Genius" comes back, oracular fashion, in a "muffled answer."

Far more successful as a consideration of the same period, as a visualization of the miracle of growth, and as an onomatopoetic description of country things is "Midsummer. (On the Farm.)." Reminiscent in point of view and circumstances of "Midsummer in the South," a poem written a decade earlier, the passages detail-

ing growth and country things are among the best Hayne wrote in
any of his late lyrics. The struggle of the seed for life in another
form is, as Whittier observed, suggested impressively:

> Meanwhile, dim forces under earth
> Are struggling blindly up to birth;
> Thro' combinations slow and strange
> Come miracles of chemic change;
> For Nature's law and Nature's life
> Blend wisely in harmonious strife.
> O! for a spirit's subtlest ear
> The stir of wakening seeds to hear!

The particulars of rural life demonstrate a knowledge of local
color and contribute to the illusion of reality the poet-speaker seeks
to create:

> Hearken from heathland haunts remote,
> The plover's melancholy note,
> Drowsed to a mild, phantasmal call,
> With flickerings of a "dying fall";
> The partridge whistling at the edge
> Of yon old tract of broom or sedge;
> The lazy beetles' languid stir,
> And boom of bees, whose lumbering whirr
> Dies quaintly, as their pinions close
> In petalled cloisters of the rose;
> Coy crickets, in the leafy dark
> Round massive boles of moss-grown bark;
> And where green coverts front the blue,
> The dove's monotonous, mournful coo,
> So weirdly sad its cadence seems
> The pensive echo of dead dreams,
> Or ghost of love's voice, breathed in sighs
> Of half Elysian memories,
> Borne—ah! with what ethereal grace!—
> From some divine, high trysting place!

Besides such passages, there are two brief choric songs in this
ode, the second of which seems especially worthy of note. Called

forth by the speaker, the "small brown bird," the dove, sings his "moan of love":

> *A bird I seem, and yet am scarce a bird!*
> *My first ancestress of the leaf and bole,*
> *(A poet thou, and hast not heard?)*
> *Held a sad woman's soul.*
> *To her by glamour of strange gods transferred*
> *A heart made dreary, dreary for love's sake,*
> *That breaking ever, still could never break;*
> *Its pulse of pain is throbbing now in mine!*
> *Hence from the muffling oak and lyric pine,*
> *Or willowy branches trailed o'er streamlets low,*
> *I make my ceaseless, "immemorial moan!"*
> *The sea prolongs it, and the haunted shore,*
>
> > *Forevermore!*
> >
> > *Forevermore!*
> >
> > *Forevermore!*

This bird is neither that of Poe nor Whitman, but the music is appropriate to the bird, and the bird to it, in a way that seems inimitable and that has the finality of art. Of course, a few fragments, even good ones, do not make an unforgettable poem; but "Midsummer" possesses qualities which show Hayne at his best. As Whittier wrote him on October 6, [1884]: "Thy 'Mid-Summer' is full of delicious poetry—passages that Marvell might have written." For one who admired, as Whittier did, "Marvell's wit and graceful song," this is a gracious compliment; but, more importantly, in this instance Hayne not only wrote good poetry but he also managed to make his style suit his materials so that the traditional and the local are brought together in such a way as to suggest both the particular and the universal.

"On a Jar of Honey," perhaps the most pleasant of the farm lyrics, is not really a "farm" poem at all. Prompted by a "present of remarkably fine honey" from Joseph Bean, an Augusta friend, the poet in nine, bright six-line stanzas considers the origin of the bees (they are "Hymettean" and Plato enjoyed their handiwork in

"Academe"), and then he contemplates the nectar itself (VII-IX):

> Your liquid amber, mixed with wine,
>   Once flushed Aspasia's heavenly face,
> When at old banquets, half-divine,
>   Mirth, Power and Genius wooed her grace;
> And o'er the board in map-capped ease,
> Jested young Alcibiades!
>
> I turn the glass, it burns and beams
>   In fire-side lustres flashed aslant,
> Until its bosomed splendor teems
>   With shapes and colors palpitant!
> Where twinkling like a wizard star,
> Smiles the quaint genius of the jar!
>
> Unsealed from out its crystal hold,
>   Let each slow, honeyed wavelet slip!
> The melted soul of sunset's gold
>   Is trembling on the perfumed lip;
> And thoughts, like charmed melodious bees,
> Sing of youth's lost Hesperides.

As always, the past casts a spell over Hayne, and he sees the present in terms of it—not so much as past is prologue but, at times, as a golden age beyond the achievement of the modern era. In this lyric the idea is not seriously advanced (indeed, the ancient bees have managed to transmit their secrets to their "latest offspring"); but even in a brief acknowledgment of a not unusual gift from a friend, Hayne cannot refrain from viewing it in the context of another day and from casting the glamour of the past over it. Still, in "Jar of Honey" the attitude expressed is neither sentimental nor mournful nor melancholic but light and wistful; and, though the poem doubtless loses some of its potential in sacrificing the local to the antique, it also gains in charm and universality.

Altogether, the nature lyrics collected in "Last Poems" contain some excellent poetry; but no single piece is completely successful in itself, unless it be the least seriously conceived of them all, "On a Jar of Honey." There are indeed fine passages in "Midsummer" and "In the Wheat Field," but these poems lack unity, esthetic distance, or the fusion of art and nature which characterizes works of more lasting significance. If there is nothing here of the scope and finish of "Unveiled" or "Muscadines," there is consolation in the substantial effort Hayne was making on relatively new material for an unaccustomed audience. Emerson might have called this an example of his doctrine of compensation, for Hayne revealed that his mind and muse were still active and that he had a sense of obligation to literature which led to a broadening of his own horizons as well as of those who read him. As R. W. Knott put it in a *Home and Farm* editorial of July 15, 1886, nine days after the poet's death: "Our readers will remember the skill and the simplicity with which he touched on the every-day life of the farm; how he dignified the labor of the husbandman; how, from the upturned sod and from the gathered harvests, he brought some thought that linked each man to all, and, for a moment at least, lifted the cloud of isolation and desolation which so desperately clings about the American farmer." Compensation, indeed, for any writer who seeks to reach the "great heart of humanity."

The religious verse brought together in the section of "Miscellaneous Poems" is of less consequence in range and in emphasis than the nature lyrics. There are merely seven brief pieces which may be considered in this category, only two of which exceed forty lines. Generally, they deal with matters of faith and death. In "Unfaith," one of the longest lyrics, the speaker (Hayne himself, of course) rails against those who exalt "Christless creeds," the fools who "grope in midnight, and still deem it morn"; since "Error and Pride" vex the souls of men with "antique problems," the poet wishes rather to pass "to pure calm" where nature and law and ancient concord rule, "where Truths we know foreshadow the Unknown," and where he may see "God's radiant face" and hear "his still voice."

"Easter," the longest of the religious poems, fixes faith more specifically on "Christ and . . . Immortality." It begins with Calvary, celebrates the meaning of the risen Lord, and concludes

> With reverent thoughts and kindling eyes,
> We view this marvellous morning rise,—
> Made lovelier by the sun-warm kiss
> Of April's *palingenesis:*
> Each new-born flower uplifts a face
> Of rapturous resurrection grace,
> And yonder strong, bright sea-waves seem
> Voices of *one* transcendent dream:—

> Sing Easter memories, sing and shine!—
> Ye make this spring-flusht hour divine
> As that far dawn in Palestine!

The most interesting religious poems, however, are two written with other topics in mind but in which faith becomes integral to the work. The earliest of these, "Closing In," appeared in *Lippincott's Magazine*, August, 1882, and is a cry for faith which preceded by only a few months Hayne's confirmation in the Episcopal Church. Beginning with the coming of "twilight shades" and sleep, the poet awaits a "funereal call" and wishes that

> even now, at this last hour,
> Faith could uplift me on a storm of power,
> Nerve the frail limbs, roll back the ebbing life,
> And whirl me to the utmost heart of strife,
> Where, from some hallowed field by heroes trod
> My soul might pass on cloud and fire to God!

The answer came soon in the resignation and acceptance of "In Harbor," a lyric written at about the same time and published a month before in *Harper's Monthly* but included in the Complete Edition (see Chapter 5 above).

Another adumbration of his faith appeared three years later in the *Sunday School Times* for December 19, 1885. Dedicated to Chancellor Lipscomb, "The Guest" describes the Methodist divine's influence on his friend.

> A charm divinely pure and bright
>   Breathed round him its ethereal calm;—
> His eyes were wells of marvellous light,—
>   His voice was like a heavenly psalm.

His example recalls to the poet's mind the "old Legend" of the "Saint of Patmos," "Our Lord's beloved Evangelist," and his words, " 'What if he tarry 'till I come?' ":

> And still he spake on solemn themes,
>   And still the glory in his eyes,
> Was that which woos the happy streams
>   And crowns the hills of Paradise!

And still I heard and still I saw,
  Till tranced my faltering lips grew dumb,—
Deep love was mine, and tender awe,—
  "What if he tarry 'till I come?"

Lipscomb, a guest on several occasions at Copse Hill, had served his host in more ways than one to bring him to an ever closer awareness of the life after death and to a surer reliance on the Christ. Hayne's own "heroic manhood," to use Lipscomb's phrase, was, in turn, a source of strength to the older man, as he acknowledged in a letter written on December 21, two days after "The Guest" appeared in print for the first time: "I often thank Providence that you came to me with so much beauty and blessing when I most needed heart and hope." A candid admission for a minister to make to a layman, but Hayne's faith had come a long way and would now find its best expression in "Face to Face" and in the impressive affirmation of the last days of his life.

The other verse of consequence in the miscellaneous section consists of one political lyric, two on literary topics, and a brief tribute to Charles Gayarré. "Columbia," the first of these, is an inauguration-day lyric published in *Harper's Weekly* for March 7, 1885. Hailing, in effect, the return of the Democrats to power, the poet sees Columbia, representing the nation, turning from a "time of blight" and discord to the "balms of peace." But Hayne's enthusiasm soon paled, as he informed Gayarré on April 29: "After 20 years I saw the *'old Democracy'* up again; & failed in my excitement to reflect that this very Party could no longer be what once it was." Such ardor is not enough to save the poem, nor is it successful even in a topical sense; for, vague and abstract, it displays Hayne's unfortunate penchant for ornate diction and personification.

The two poems on literary topics exhibit some of these same weaknesses and others besides. "The Ivory Gate (A Lyric for Poets)," purchased by the *Christian Union* in October, 1884, too consciously levies upon literary legend and then too conventionally draws an analogy in the last stanza between thoughts and dreams. It smells of the lamp, and its companion piece, "Literary Immortality," maintains that not only does such enduring fame seem limited before "dread millenniums" (even Shakespeare's glorious song when "matched with the ages" may lose its quality) but also that "earthly immortality" may make angels "smile in irony."

A better poem in thought and workmanship than any of these is "Charles Gayarré." Coming as it does at the end of Hayne's long, three-part essay on his friend in the *Southern Bivouac* for June, July, and August, 1886, the poem serves at once as a climax to the article and as a tribute to the character of the man. The sonnet-like structure presents to good advantage the poet's view of his friend's duality ("imperial resolution" on the one hand and "gracious tenderness" on the other), and the lines of blank verse provide an appropriate objectivity of tone and dignity of movement. Surely Milton's tailed sonnet offered at least a precedent in length, and the Shakespearean form suggested the couplet at the end:

> A man of ample brain and lofty spirit,
> No storms of doom can baffle or subdue;
> Who as he took fair fortune gratefully,
> Now fronts the tempest like a mighty tower
> Four-square to all the winds; no prop gives way,
> No buttressed wall sinks crumbling to the ground,
> No 'coign of vantage' yields, no stone is hurled
> To base from battlement, while over all
> Imperial resolution, undismayed,
> Glows like a banner 'gainst the sunset clouds.
> But ah! within that steadfast nature beats
> A human heart, all gracious tenderness,
> As at the core of some vast granite rock,
> Only revealed to the deep glance of heaven,
> Shines a strange fountain, beautiful as dawn,
> And full of gentle murmurings as a dream,
> When Love, descending, stirs the golden deep,
> And music rises from the soul of sleep!

These lines are among the last Hayne ever wrote. They did not appear until after his death, but they constitute the most serious and effective effort he ever made to adjust a standard literary type to his own creative needs. Whatever their ultimate literary value, they represent an innovation in technique for him; and they characterize very well indeed the Charles Gayarré he knew and admired.

VII *Sonnets*

Though Hayne did not compose many sonnets during the last years of his life, fifteen are collected here—and some of these are as good as any of his earlier efforts in this form. For convenience of discussion, they are divided into four groups—those on political topics, those dealing with prominent men (several of these might be included in the first category), those on the seasons, and those on his own life.

The political sonnets are three in number, and they express generally the political views Hayne maintained consistently throughout the postwar period. Though "To the New South," for example, first appeared in 1885 in two publications usually friendly to New South sentiments—the New Orleans *Times-Democrat* and the Atlanta magazine *Dixie*—Hayne's poem is actually a compliment to the Old South. Acknowledging the "radiant rise" of the New South's sun and the "sunset" of the Old, the poet nevertheless devotes the sestet to the latter:

> How oft is sunset beautiful and grand!
> Its very clouds are steeped in light and grace,
> The glow and pathos of a farewell time—
> 'Tis thence the Past uplifts her dying face,
> And if that Past hath been like *ours* sublime,
> Oh! Show her reverence in the sunset-land!

The same general theme runs through the other political lyrics. "The Renegade" in particular is a bitter attack on those whom Hayne considered to be turncoats to the Lost Cause; and though subtitled "Suggested by a Painting of Kaulbach's in Munich" in the *Independent* for January 22, 1885, it is obviously directed at George W. Cable, as Hayne indicated in a letter to Mrs. Preston of December 16, 1884: "Mr. Cable is pleased to remark in his last novel that everybody South now 'execrates the idea of Slavery' (or words to that effect); and altogether undertakes to be spokesman, the miserable little ci-devant clerk & parvenu, a thorough Yankee in blood, wherever, by accident, he was born, for this entire section of Country, touching past political beliefs & principles, of which he knows evidently next to nothing (!!). . . . Here is a Sonnet which explains itself—":

> A glorious Cause! . . true! . . but the Cause lies dead,
> Most like an outstretched Titan, gaunt & pale—,
> Most awful, sightless eyes, & shattered mail,—
> Lax limbs supine, & earth-recumbent head:

O! kingly form, no more disquieted;—
　　While loyal thousands His dark doom bewail,—
　　One traitorous knave hath only tongue to rail,
And mock the vows his own false lips had said:—
　　How *once* he feigned, yea, flattered, fawned & lied,
For gifts that shone in that frank, liberal hand;—
　　Now, for spent blessing, his dead Lord is banned:—
　　Past blindness mourned, his "mea culpa" cried:—
　　Blithely he joins the Conqueror's proud "command"—,
And—Stentor—Judas—, shouts on victory's side!

There were, however, men who kept the faith, B. H. Hill and
Robert E. Lee among them; and Hayne expressed his approbation
of their integrity and courage. "Fronting the Shadow" honors Hill's
oratory and statesmanship, but stresses especially his religious faith;
and "Robert Lee" (*Southern Bivouac*, February, 1886) stands as a
model of Hayne's achievement in the form as well as a declaration
of what he admired in the man:

　　Defeat but made him tower more grandly high—
　　Sackcloth about *him* was transformed to gold
　　And royal purple, in each flawless fold;
　　His soul pierced darkness like the sun-god's eye;
　　His the deep knowledge how to live, and die.
　　Calmly benignant, and superbly bold,
　　All incorruptible—unbought, unsold—
　　A steadfast splendor in a stormy sky.
　　The winds may rage, the frightened clouds be driven
　　Like multitudinous banners, torn and tossed,
　　Retreating from some mighty conflict lost—
　　But, far beyond all shapes and sounds of ill,
　　That star—his soul—is shining calmly still,
　　A steadfast splendor in a stormy heaven!

Two other sonnets complimenting prominent men were addressed
to old friends, John Greenleaf Whittier and R. D. Blackmore. The
tribute to the Quaker poet, the last of four directed to him, illustrates Hayne's affection for the man and his respect for the "pure
grandeur" of his character. The basic figure is that of a "lonely

pine" as the "type" of Whittier's "poet soul." The sestet follows:

> Type of thy soul is he—thy poet soul;
>   His spell transforms the storm-winds into song,
> That, charmed in sweeping rhythmic branch and bole,
>   Lapse to the long low music of the sea;
> While birds, like the winged Hopes, furled from wintry wrong,
>   Dream of spring heavens in that deep-hearted tree!

Composed on a "stormy morning in January, 1885," and published in *Harper's Weekly* for February 27, 1886, the poem is a gracious compliment to an old friend who quickly returned his thanks "for the kind and beautiful words of thy sonnet."

The sonnet to Blackmore, written a few weeks earlier (December 10, 1884), also seeks to characterize the man and his work but in more particular terms. The author of *Lorna Doone* is "friend to the world and me" and "teacher . . . guide and sweet philosopher." "Touched" by Shakespeare and "toned by Verulam," he is a "prose Chaucer . . . whom all Nature's loves embrace." To present readers, this tribute may sound too flattering, but Blackmore was considered in the 1880's an important novelist on both sides of the Atlantic, and the friendship between the two writers was warm and sincere, as witness the Englishman's dedication of his *Springhaven* (1887) to Hayne and his remarks to Mrs. Hayne regarding the poet's death, written two years after that event: "Which of us shall leave a name so worthy to be held sacred? I was reading one of his old letters, only the other day, & the greatness of his nature made me grieve that I am not like him. Little jerks of thought, & dismal doubt, are so ignominious, in the clear sunlight of a large bright soul."[5]

A "sunlight" of another sort finds expression in Hayne's sonnets on the seasons, especially in "April" (*Christian Union*, April 20, 1882); and, though the others deal with November and winter, they also manifest a longing amid the "snarling gusts" and "serpent-darkness" of the wintry world for the "bright empire" of "summer's grace." April itself is renewal, a "magical maiden" from a "realm unknown"

> Beyond our mortal lands, and mortal seas,
>   What isle of yet undreamed Hesperides,
> Com'st thou on wings from fragrant spaces blown,

With white feet winged, and flower-compassed zone—
   Fair spirit of balm and beauty, beam and breeze,
   Of changeful hues, and haunting harmonies—
To claim 'twixt heaven and earth thy sapphire throne?
Ah! whenceso'er this rosy wanderer came,
   Hers the rare glory and voluptuous grace
Which touched the earth's first poet heart to flame;
   And so shall flush her last—when all aglow,
Fresh as of old, she lifts her marvelous face
   Above some final spring-tide's golden flow!

Neither cruel nor the bringer of sweet showers, April is then the eternal female who comes to inspire and inflame the earth in season and to return "fresh as of old" until the end comes in "some final spring-tide." A touch erotic, perhaps, for the usually chaste poet, but the "flower-compassed zone" and "voluptuous grace" of the "rosy wanderer" who touches "the earth's first poet heart to flame" are too obvious to overlook even if other aspects are so nebulously suggested by diction and rhythm as to leave the reader aware of the possibilities but wondering about his own imagination.

The three personal sonnets are generally more interesting as revelations of Hayne's attitudes and opinions than as successful lyrics, though "Death's Self" may be a partial exception to this evaluation. The other two—"Written upon the Night of December 31 [1885], near Midnight" and "Upon My 56th Birthday"—are complementary in thought and are prompted by the turn of the year, the poet's birthday occurring on January 1. The first decries man's misuse of time, and the second acknowledges, amidst the "ghosts of perished years," the coming on of the "Twilight" years.

The best poem of this lot, however, is "Death's Self," originally "The Thought of Death," as it was called in a manuscript version sent to Lipscomb in the spring of 1885:

The thought of death walks ever by my side,
   It walks in sunshine, and it walks in shade,
   A thing protean, by strange fancies made
Lovely or loathsome, dark or glorified.
But past such fantasies Death's self must hide,
   While his dread hour to smite is still delayed,
   Like a masked Presence in a cypress glade,
By all save heaven's keen vision undescried.

> For me what final aspect shalt thou take,
>   O Death? Or shalt thou take no shape at all,
>   But viewless, soundless, on my spirit fall,
>   Soft as the sleep-balm of a summer's night,
> From which the flower-like soul, new-born, shall wake
> In God's fair gardens on the hills of light?

The prospect of death as dreadful or gentle is not new with Hayne—indeed, as in Whitman's "When Lilacs Last in the Dooryard Bloom'd," the thought of death walks by the protagonist's side; but the knowledge of death remains unresolved in the sonnet. Of course the parallel is not exact in other ways because Hayne does not interpret death as Whitman does, but it is worth noting that poets so widely divergent in their theory and practice could on occasion approach community in the treatment of an important idea. In this instance, the similarity is more thought-provoking than usual since Whitman was not aware of Hayne at all and Hayne, as noted earlier, was vehemently opposed to almost everything Whitman stood for as man and poet.

Altogether, the last sonnets show no great advance over earlier ones in regard to thought, but structure is a different matter. Hayne is still the careful and conscious craftsman. He concentrates on the basic Italian form, varying it chiefly in the sestet, though in four octaves (see, for example, the one addressed to Blackmore), he follows Wordsworth's example in changing the usual rhyme scheme of *abbaabba* to *abbaacca*. The sestet patterns, however, are seldom the same. In fifteen poems (actually seventeen since two are double sonnets) there are fourteen different arrangements of rhyme in the sestet; but all retain the integrity of the six-line unit, even the two that end with couplets. In this way Hayne achieves a measure of variety without resorting to the English form, and the occurrence of rhyme is handled so as to contrast with the regularity of the octave and to suggest an independence from rhyme since it is not so noticeable as in the three common sestet sequences.

As a whole, these sonnets, together with those of his earlier collections, should entitle Hayne to serious consideration as a practitioner of a form too demanding for some and surely not widely employed by many nineteenth-century American poets. Aside from Longfellow and possibly one or two others, Hayne is the most substantial sonneteer of the period.

VIII *Quatrains*

In the last three years of his life Hayne began composing quatrains, a stanza form he had used throughout his career but hardly
ever as an entity in itself. He wrote Lipscomb about his work on
February 29, 1884, and enclosed a few examples to illustrate his
theories: "The Quatrain," he avers, "ought to be of two sorts, 1*stly*
Four lines which embrace an original or partly original Thought,
or fancy, tersely expressed; 2*ndly* Four lines which even if the
Thought, or fancy, is unoriginal are made pleasing to the Reader
by means of adroit metrical execution."

Proceeding on this basis, Hayne created lyrics on many of his
usual topics—nature, love, politics, religion, and death—and published them in the magazines and newspapers. Still, despite his
obvious attraction to the epigrammatic nature of the form, he was
aware of its limitations; and he warned Will in a letter of March 9,
1885, to eschew the "four-lined pieces" in favor of longer "lyrics of
from 3 to half a dozen stanzas."

Thirty-six of these brief lyrics are brought together in this section. Several may be quoted to represent Hayne's contribution in
this vein. "May," for example, offers a characteristic thought and
figure:

> All maiden lives that waned in their young prime—
> Since the first beating of the heart of Time—
> Re-live, I dream, in May's mysterious grace,
> Sing through her birds and blossom in her face.

" 'And God Fulfills Himself in Many Ways' " echoes Tennyson,
as the epigraph makes plain but with a twist:

> If God fulfills Himself in many ways
> Through the slow change of our nights and days,
> Dream not that Satan's maimed on some dark shelf,
> He, too, in countless ways fulfills himself.

Also Tennysonian in point of departure at least are " 'The Old
Order Changeth' ":

> The old order changing, giving place to new,
> Bequeaths us *something* noble, stainless, true.
> Thus, while it crumbles, lost in mold and rust,
> Hoard the pure gold which sanctifies its dust.

And "Faith in Conflict":

> Souls! gently raised to mountain-heights of Trust,
> Scorn *not* your brethren, battling in the vale,—
> For noblest faith, Antaean, springs from dust,—
> The grandest warrior comes with battered mail!

With or without Tennyson's precedent Hayne held these ideas sincerely and consistently and was not merely indebted to the English laureate for them. His notions regarding old orders, for example, he surely imbibed in the beginning from his Uncle Robert; and his almost lifelong struggle for faith led, as he suggests in "Second Birth," to the crystallization of a view more peculiar to Hayne than to Tennyson:

> A realm there is on earth, yet not of earth—
> A kingdom wider than all land and sea;
> Only thro' travail of man's second birth,
> Our souls may find that kingdom's golden key!

Whatever the ultimate poetic value of these verses (and Hayne is more at home with "adroit metrical execution" than with "original Thought" or terseness of expression), they compose an addition to the corpus of Hayne's work which, like the farm poems and the tribute to Gayarré, show that the poet was willing and able even at "the eleventh hour," as he put it on several occasions, to undertake something different or to make a new approach to something old and familiar. This characteristic is perhaps a key to any evaluation of Hayne as poet. He was willing to try most of the traditional forms, and he could handle many of them with ease and facility (particularly lyrics and sonnets); but he had not the genius to make any of them truly, inevitably, and finally his own.

CHAPTER 7

A Summing Up[1]

HAYNE'S limitations as a poet are clear, but they were not so obvious in his own day. He was considered by many competent judges—Longfellow, Whittier, Holmes, Whipple, Stedman, Thompson, Lanier, Cooke, Mrs. Preston, Tennyson, Marston, Blackmore, and Collins, among them—to be an important American poet. Whittier, for example, wrote Mrs. Hayne shortly after her husband's death that he was assured a place in the "Valhalla of the country" along with Longfellow, Bryant, and Taylor. Those who characterized Hayne as a minor bard seldom maintained that his place as such was not secure and lasting. Yet today Hayne's poetry is largely neglected and unread except, perhaps, in college courses in Southern literature and in some surveys of American literature. A recent anthology of nineteenth-century American poetry that is purportedly representative does not offer his work, but poets of considerably lower stature are included.[2]

There are of course many reasons for the decline of Hayne's reputation, but the emphasis in this summation is on the weaknesses of his poetry, especially as regards its derivative nature, lack of intellectual force and vigor, and its failure to express adequately the substance of life. These are so closely related as to make any discussion of each seem arbitrary, but a brief examination of each in turn may be illuminating.

A random reading of any of Hayne's volumes reveals immediately his debt to English poetic tradition, a body of ideas, materials, and precedents he accepted and appropriated gladly and which he thought so basic that anyone (Whitman, for example) who ignored or attacked it was "mad." His own work, early and late, owes much to Spenser, Scott, Hunt, Shelley, Keats, Poe, and Tennyson. Shakespeare and Milton he acknowledges as masters, but their influence is less pervasive than that of the nineteenth-century poets. After the Civil War, Chaucer, Wordsworth, Morris, and Longfellow provided certain standards and served as congenial guides. A "belated Romanticist," as both Hubbell and Parks have observed, Hayne frequently expresses directly or indirectly in his poetry the worst aspects of a sterile Romanticism. It is sentimental and unabashedly personal. He hardly ever manages to keep himself out of his poems or even realizes that such a thing may be desirable. Furthermore, though he occasionally warned others of the dangers of rhyme (surprisingly enough, he found "unrhymed measures" at times "sweet" to his ears), his own verse often suffers from too much of it.

Even more damaging is the lack of intellectual content in Hayne's poems. His ideas are conventional, his views are traditional, and they are phrased usually so that little new in the way of insight or fresh in the way of interpretation seems evident. Though he read widely and long and was acquainted with developments in literature, politics, philosophy, and religion, Hayne's mind was not a deep one; and his poetry accordingly seldom achieves profundity. He was, to be sure, capable of deep feeling, but only infrequently does he manage to convey it fully and successfully in a poem. He was profoundly moved, for example, by the postwar situation of the South; and, in the last years of his life, by the human condition in regard to death and immortality; but the best expression of his views on these questions appears in his letters to Gayarré, Lipscomb, and Mrs. Preston—not in his poetry generally.

For these reasons and others his poetry often seems divorced from life despite its very personal nature. His poems often are cries of the heart against the exigencies of living, but they are couched in such diction and put in such form as to smack of the lamp rather than of life. Many belong to what may be called, after Shelley, the "falling on the thorns of life" school and suggest pose as contrasted with reality. This is of course ironic since Hayne did lose home and status in the war and did suffer from poverty and want thereafter. But, by too blatantly parading the pageant of his bleeding heart (to paraphrase Arnold), his poems frequently take on a plaintive and petulant air and fail to achieve sufficient illusion of reality to lure the reader to suspend his disbelief. Nor was his technique flexible enough to establish, by means of point of view or persona, adequate distance between poet and poem and audience to give his plight reality by rendering it objectively.

To say this much about the weaknesses of Hayne's poetry is not to say everything. A more general catalogue would include, among others, a point of view too restricted in outlook and failures in artistry resulting from a reluctance to prune or revise or eliminate.

On the other hand, a case can be made for Hayne; and, paradoxically, some of the strengths of his poetry are related to its weaknesses. His work does derive some nourishment from its sources. Chaucer, Spenser, Wordsworth, Shelley, Keats, and Tennyson, to name only a few of the best, are worthy models and offer the lesser artist much in the way of precept and technique, as is clear in "The Wife of Brittany" or in "Unveiled." And Hayne's treatment of his own locality and situation discloses at times an authenticity of detail and sincerity of emotion, as in "A Summer Mood," "Midsummer in the South," or "South Carolina to the States of the North."

Moreover, Hayne was a rather versatile versifier. He employed competently a wide range of forms, metrical schemes, and techniques. He is at his best in short poems, in sonnets such as those on Lee and Swinburne and "Carolina" and in lyrics like the Copse Hill nature pieces, "In Harbor" and "Face to Face." He can also write longer poems, odes and narratives of the quality of "Cambyses and the Macrobian Bow," "Muscadines," "Unveiled," and "The Wife of Brittany" and dramatic and meditative verses like "Vicksburg," "Fire Pictures," "By the Grave of Henry Timrod," and "The Broken Battalions."

In the scope, versatility, and bulk of his production, indeed, he is the most substantial Southern poet of the nineteenth century, a judgment which elucidates Stedman's remark concerning the "dimensions" of Hayne's "life-long work," though there is no denying that a large part of the bulk needs reducing and refining. Hayne did not write any one poem which comes near the perfection of Poe's "To Helen" or Timrod's "Ode," but he wrote *more passably good verse* than Poe or Timrod or Lanier, though it should be remembered that his career lasted half a generation longer than theirs. Hayne lacked Poe's sense of art and critical acumen, Timrod's theme and control, and Lanier's inventiveness and fertility; but he could, on occasion, be as musical as Poe, as eloquent as Timrod, and as lush as Lanier. Poe and Timrod are better poets than Hayne, if only their best work is selected to compare with his. This is not necessarily the case with Lanier, for his best is in many ways very much like Hayne's: in few instances is the promise fulfilled in the performance. Still, Hayne's canon is rounded in ways that Poe's or Timrod's or Lanier's is not. It reflects the full scope of a striving for expression in a spectrum of poetic types and structures, and it suggests therefore a range and completeness which are missing in the output of the three other nineteenth-century Southern poets of consequence. In the final analysis, however, Hayne's best poetry has not stood the test of time as well as Poe's or Timrod's or Lanier's, nor is it likely to supplant their work in the anthologies or in the minds of scholars or general readers.

Aside from the poetry of his Southern contemporaries, Hayne's may properly be considered along with that of Stedman, Stoddard, Aldrich, Boker, and Taylor, though in the 1880's there was a disposition on the part of some qualified critics to rank him with Whittier, Holmes, and Bryant. Time has not been generous to any of these poets, and Hayne now clearly belongs with Stedman and the others beneath even the modest ledge on Parnassus still occupied by Whittier, Holmes, and Bryant. Such a judgment should, of course, in no way detract from the valiant effort Hayne made from the pine barrens to be heard throughout the land nor from the dedicated devotion he paid his muse amidst discouraging and distressing conditions of poverty and ill health. It is obvious that he failed to write great poetry, but it is worth pondering that he managed to write poetry of any distinction at all.

Hayne himself recognized his limitations and accepted them. He knew early in his career that his song would not reach the heights where the "great Poets" sing, but he also realized that through poetry he could catch "brief glimpses of a life divine" and see "beyond the veil that guards the inmost shrine." Years later, echoing Coleridge, he confided to Mrs. Preston: " 'Poetry has been to me its own exceeding *great reward.*' " Who can say even now that he was not justified in singing his own songs, however minor they might be; for, besides catching glimpses of the "inmost shrine," he observed to his old friend: "Through poetic thought spiritualized, we pass from earth to heaven!"

Notes and References

(Strict limitations of space imposed by the series have forced me to pare documentation, but I have considerable additional information which I shall be glad to share with others in the field.)

Chapter One

1. This chapter appeared in a shorter and different form in the *Georgia Review* (Spring, 1968).

2. *A Collection of Hayne Letters,* ed. D. M. McKeithan (Austin, Texas, 1944), p. 399. Cited hereafter as *Letters.*

3. For a brief account of *Russell's,* see Hayne's "Ante-Bellum Charleston," *Southern Bivouac,* n.s. I (November, 1885), 330. He persists in declaring that the magazine died with the publication of the fourth volume, but *Russell's* was published for three years, a total of six volumes. With the exception of periods of illness or absence from Charleston, Hayne edited "maga" until its demise in 1860. See, for example, *Letters,* 85.

4. The correspondence concerning these visits is in J. B. Hubbell, ed., *The Last Years of Henry Timrod* (Durham, 1941), pp. 81-92 (cited hereafter as Hubbell, *Last Years*); Mary C. Simms Oliphant and others, eds., *The Letters of William Gilmore Simms* (Columbia, S.C., 1952–56), V. 3; and Hayne's "Ante-Bellum Charleston" (October, 1885), 267. Timrod died on October 7, 1867; Simms on June 11, 1870.

5. For Hayne's contributions to five monthlies, see my unpublished Ph.D. dissertation "Southern Writers and Northern Literary Magazines, 1865–1890" (Duke University, 1956); for his work in Southern journals, see Ray M. Atchison's unpublished Ph.D. dissertation, "Southern Literary Magazines, 1865–1887" (Duke University, 1956).

6. For Hayne's friendship and correspondence with Gayarré and Collins, see Charles R. Anderson, "Charles Gayarré and Paul Hayne: The Last Literary Cavaliers," *American Studies in Honor of William Kenneth Boyd,* ed. D. K. Jackson (Durham, 1940), pp. 221-81; and William Hamilton Hayne, ed., "Some Unpublished Letters of Wilkie

Collins," *The Bookman,* XXXVII (March, 1913), 66-71. There has hitherto been no treatment of the Hayne-Lipscomb friendship.

7. For accounts of Hayne's death and funeral, see the Augusta *Evening News,* July 8, 10 and the Augusta *Chronicle,* July 13. J. A. Hill, a friend and neighbor, wrote articles on Hayne's last days for the *Sunday School Times,* August 21, 1886, and the *Independent,* August 19, 1886. Other notices appeared in the Boston *Evening Transcript,* July 8, 1886; the New York *Times,* July 10, 1886; and *Harper's Weekly,* July 17, 1886.

8. Edwin M. Bacon, editor of the Boston *Post,* quoted in a letter of July 14, 1886, from Milton W. Saffold to Richard F. Michel, Mrs. Hayne's brother, in the Hayne Papers, Duke University Library. Hereafter abbreviated HP, DUL. Hayne manuscript materials (especially letters and poems) referred to in the text or notes but not cited by location may be found in this collection. Other manuscript holdings are noted and identified by institution.

9. See Hayne's letters to Stoddard, John R. Thompson, Simms, and Moses C. Tyler of August 24, 1855, October 4, 1869, December 28, 1869, and February 26, 1874 in *Letters,* 12-13, 133, 225, 324-26. See also E. W. Parks, "When Paul Hamilton Hayne Fought a Duel," *Georgia Review,* XI (Spring, 1957), 1-5.

Chapter Two

1. Hayne never collected the tribute to Butler, but it has been reprinted by Richard B. Davis in the *South Carolina Historical and Genealogical Magazine,* LII (January, 1951), 52.

2. These poems appeared in *Richards' Weekly Gazette* (later *Southern Literary Gazette*) in 1849: June 16, June 23, and November 3, From 1848 to 1864 Hayne placed fifty items in the *Messenger.*

3. Of all these pieces, only two sonnets were later collected in *Poems,* Complete Edition (1882). Cited hereafter as Complete Edition.

4. Although Stoddard found "grave faults" in "Avolio," Lowell considered it the best poem in the volume. "The subject," he observed in an *Atlantic* review in January, 1860, "is an imaginative one,—and the choice of subjects is one great test of genuine aptitude and ability. In this poem . . . Mr. Hayne shows a genuine vigor of expression and maturity of purpose."

5. This ode is one of the first of Hayne's occasional poems written in behalf of various institutions or causes. Delivered by the poet himself on February 10, 1859, the date is erroneously given as 1856 in the Complete Edition.

6. This passage, Section VII in the *Avolio* text, is omitted in later revisions. The deletion does little esthetic harm to the ode, but it

does render the anticipations of Whitman and Lanier less susceptible to critical study and scrutiny.

7. On December 28, 1859, Hayne wrote Lowell thanking him for the "indulgent & kindly notice" and promising to profit from the "counsel so kindly given" (*Letters*, 99-100).

8. *Letters*, 131. For other reprintings of war poems, see James E. Routh, Jr., "Some Fugitive Poems by Paul Hamilton Hayne," *South Atlantic Quarterly*, IX (October, 1910), 327-33, and "Two Fugitive Poems of Paul Hamilton Hayne," *Journal of English and Germanic Philology*, XVII, No. 3 (1918), 426-29.

9. With the exception of "The Kentucky Partisan" and "Butler's Proclamation," both of which are reprinted by Routh, these poems are collected in the Complete Edition. All citations are from these sources. In editing these pieces in 1882 Hayne eliminated some of the bitter feeling expressed in them earlier.

Two of Hayne's most interesting poems of this period—"The Southern Lyre" and "The Wife of Brittany"—have little to do with the war. The first of these, a treatment of Southern poets in the style but without the wit of Lowell's "Fable for Critics," has lately been reprinted by Richard B. Harwell in *American Literature*, XXIV (March, 1952), 51-61. The second, a redaction of one of the *Canterbury Tales*, is the subject of a full-scale discussion by Edd W. Parks in *Essays in Honor of Walter Clyde Curry* (Nashville, 1955), 103-15.

10. This poem appeared in the Charleston *Mercury*, March 18, 1862. Hayne added a note in which he explained that the piece had been "composed" before Timrod's "noble lyric (on 'Carolina')" had appeared. See also Hubbell's *Last Years*, p. 20.

11. April 8, 1870. The original is in HP, DUL, and is quoted in *Last Years*, pp. 116-17. Holmes had praised the poem earlier on November 4, 1866. Original in HP, DUL. The poem originally was called "Lee Crossing the Potomac" and appeared in the Charleston *Mercury* for September 26, 1862.

12. Charleston *Daily Courier*, March 24, 1862. See also T. Harry Williams, *P. G. T. Beauregard: Napoleon in Gray* (Baton Rouge, 1954), pp. 122-23.

13. A note appended to the poem quotes an eyewitness as reporting that "some weeks after the beginning" of the bombardment that "not only were ladies seen coolly walking the streets, but that . . . children were observed at play." The poem has more recently appeared in *Poems of American History*, ed. Burton E. Stevenson (1922); Edd Winfield Parks, ed., *Southern Poets* (1936); and Richmond C. Beatty and others, eds., *The Literature of the South* (1952). In the first of these anthologies, Stevenson, by placing the ballad in the chronology for 1863, contributes to the common mistaken notion that it deals with Grant's siege of Vicksburg in that year.

14. Printed in the Charleston *Mercury* for May 26, 1862, this piece may now be more readily found in Routh's article in the *South Atlantic Quarterly* or in *Poems of American History*. In 1883, Hayne paid his respects again to "Old Butler the Beast" in an incomplete and untitled poem published by H. Blair Rouse and Floyd C. Watkins in "Some Manuscript Poems by Paul Hamilton Hayne," *Emory University Quarterly*, VIII (June, 1952), 83-91.

15. The letter to Stoddard is printed by Harry Shaw, Jr., in *American Literature*, IV (May, 1932), 195-99. The remarks on war are contained in a letter of June 15 [1885?] to W. A. Courtenay in the South Caroliniana Library, University of South Carolina.

Chapter Three

1. In his diary for August 25, 1864, Hayne recorded: "(This day the steamer FOX sailed for Liverpool. My letter & poems went by her!)."

On August 9, 1864, Hayne informed Dr. Francis Peyre Porcher that he had "written quite enough [since 1861] to fill a good-sized duodecimo vol. of verses." Quoted from the original in the South Caroliniana Library; not included among the seven letters of Hayne to Porcher printed by Richard B. Davis in *Studies in Philology*, XLIV (July, 1947), 529-48.

2. Hayne was not pleased with his arrangements with the Lippincott firm. One of the reasons he went north in 1873 was to check on the sales of *Legends and Lyrics* at the home office in Philadelphia. He wrote his wife on July 13: "How do you think the Lippincotts have treated me? After the sale of the 'stereotype-plates,' etc., they made out that the *balance* in my favor amounts to *only Five* DOLLARS!! . . . They are scamps!! complete scamps!!"

3. The original is in the John R. Thompson Papers, Alderman Library, University of Virginia.

4. "Hayne's Adaptation of Chaucer's Franklin's Tale," p. 115.

5. Lanier's letter is in the Centennial Edition of his *Works*, ed. Charles R. Anderson and others, 1945, VIII, 133-34. The essay is reprinted in *Works*, V, 322-33. Hayne was not pleased by some of Lanier's criticism and wrote Mrs. Preston on January 25, 1875, defending "The Wife of Brittany" against Lanier's assertion that the passion of such poems was a mere "titillation of the unreal."

6. Whipple's review appeared in the Boston *Evening Transcript*, February 5, 1872; Stoddard's in the *Aldine*, V (March, 1872), 68; and Mrs. Preston's in the *Southern Magazine*, n.s. III (March, 1872), 377-81.

7. *The South in American Literature, 1607–1900* (Durham, 1954), p. 757. Cited hereafter as *S.A.L.*

8. In the John R. Thompson Papers, Alderman Library, University of Virginia. "Under the Pine" appeared first in *Lippincott's*, II (October, 1868), 414-16.

9. The poem appeared in *Southern Society* in the last issue of December, 1867, and Hayne received thirty dollars for it. Later, after the Chicago fire of 1871, a revised version came out in *Harper's Weekly*, XV (November 11, 1871), 1066, and it was reprinted in *The Illustrated Newspaper*, London, November 25, 1871. In the meantime Lanier had read the ms and criticized it in a letter of March 20, 1871 (*Works*, VIII, 145-48). The text in *Legends and Lyrics* includes an additional strophe beginning "Titan arches! Titan spires!" Though the title is spelled variously "Fire-Pictures" or "Fire Pictures" in Hayne's letters and in the Complete Edition, the spelling used in *Legends and Lyrics* is "Fire Pictures."

10. The text of "The Bells" is that given in the *Union Magazine* for December, 1849. This version, as Killis Campbell points ont in his edition of Poe's *Poems* (1917; rep., 1962), "differs radically from the final text" (p. 123n.).

11. After explaining on February 1, 1872, that she had tempered her praise in her review in order to avoid the editorial blue pencil, Mrs. Preston added: "Now let me tell you how *admirable* I think *Lyrics & Legends [sic]*—it is the truest book of poems that has ever come from a Southern singer. There is none in the range of my knowledge that can compare with it in fine, polished artistic work— real poet-work."

12. *The Correspondence of Bayard Taylor and Paul Hamilton Hayne*, ed. Charles Duffy (Baton Rouge, 1945), pp. 51-52. Cited hereafter as *Corres. of Taylor and Hayne*.

Chapter Four

1. The letter to Stoddard is in the A. L. Hench Collection, Alderman Library, University of Virginia, and the one to James is printed in *Letters*, 418. Despite Hayne's opinion, the poem is included with very little change or revision in the Complete Edition.

2. The "power" of Hayne's poetry, observed a reviewer in the Boston *Daily Advertiser* (n.d., clipping, HP, DUL), "is in its intensity of feeling, rather than its loftiness of thought. We would not be understood to intimate that it lacks intellectual strength; but the thought, however high and true, is always softened, refined, and graced by other qualities that constitute its poetic worth."

3. Since Hayne considered Whitman a wretched poet and vulgar man, he is not likely to have read "Lilacs" nor to have used it in any way even if he had known the poem. For his opinion of Whit-

man, see various letters of the 1870's to A. H. Dooley, F. S. Saltus, and Edgar Fawcett in HP, DUL. He wrote Dooley, an Indiana bookseller and admirer, on March 8, 1876: "I have not seen Walt Whitman's new book; nor, to be frank, do I care a 'button' about it! The world, or rather a few artists, English & American, have gone mad, touching the characteristics of this odd writer. One thing is certain: if Mr. Walt Whitman really is in any sense or to any degree, a genuine Poet; then, all the canons of poetic art must be reversed; and their most illustrious expounders be consigned to oblivion, from Job to Homer; from Homer to Horace; from Horace to Shakspeare; from Shakspeare to Tennyson."

4. See "Out of the Cradle Endlessly Rocking" and "A Route of Evanescence." Another poem which evokes the Dickinson lyric is "Our 'Humming Bird,'" a delicate treatment of the capricious and bewitching bird in an intricate stanza rhyming *abccbdde*, the first line stating a rhyme which is echoed in the initial line of each succeeding stanza, and the last line of the first, a four-syllable modified refrain, establishes a similar pattern for the remaining four stanzas and serves as a tail to each one.

5. *The Mountain of the Lovers* was widely reviewed. See, for example, Maurice Thompson's article in the Indianapolis *Journal*, May 29, 1875; E. P. Whipple's in the Boston *Evening Transcript*, June 22, 1875; James A. Harrison's in the *Southern Magazine* for September, 1875; James Barron Hope's in the Norfolk *Landmark* (n.d., clipping, HP, DUL); and W. D. Howells' in the *Atlantic* for October, 1875. Anonymous reviews appeared in the Boston *Daily Advertiser* (n.d., clipping, HP, DUL); *Appletons' Journal* for June 26, 1875; the *Christian Union* for July 14, 1875; the *Aldine* for September, 1875; and *Scribner's Monthly* for September, 1875.

6. Still Hayne maintained to Charles Gayarré on July 7, 1885, "even thus 'cabbined [*sic*], cribbed, confined,' the genuine artist is true to himself, & his vocation! His humblest 'literary calico' may be threaded with gold; & from the 'Inkstand of the Devil' may magically come some glittering drops, drawn from the very heart's blood of Apollo!"

Chapter Five

1. *Letters*, 399. The inaccuracies, Hayne explained to Mrs. Preston on October 21, 1882, were the result of the firm's decision to read proof itself: "Not a *solitary proof sheet* could I see, the Lothrops saying it would be inconvenient to send them so far; and declaring moreover their own proof readers to be *experts (!!)*" Aside from many minor typographical errors, the proem to "Daphles" was omitted;

the poems from *The Mountain of the Lovers* were placed under the *Legends and Lyrics* rubric and the dedications to both volumes were left out; and Hayne's instructions that the "adult portion of the Book" end with "The Pole of Death" and "In Harbor" and that the section of poems for children be concluded with "Old Geoffrey's Relic" were ignored.

2. To include such verse was in itself assertion enough, at least to Maurice Thompson, who wrote frankly on March 15, 1883: "You are fully appreciated at the North, Hayne, and I hope you will not injure your growing influence by any more bitter war-poems. I am in a position to know that such writings will retard and hinder your just recognition as a *national* poet. You must not permit yourself to become *sectional* or *local*. . . . Forget, as a poet, that there ever was a so-called Confederacy. A poet must have wide visions, and you have. You are a noble poet, and I wish to see you take your true place."

3. "The Pine's Mystery" came out in *Baldwin's Monthly*, XVIII (February, 1879) and "The Fallen Pine-Cone" in the *Independent*, XXXII (September 23, 1880). Though "The Dryad of the Pine" presumably was published in April or May, 1880, in *Andrews' American Queen*, I have not been able to examine the appropriate issues.

4. *Harper's Bazar*, XIII (March 6, 1880), 150. The title in the *Bazar* is "To a Bee. (In the Florida Woods.).," and the author's name is not given, but the poem is clearly Hayne's. Aside from a few later changes, the text is that of the Complete Edition.

5. See, for example, his letters to Mrs. Preston of April 17, 1870, and August 29, 1871; to Francis O. Ticknor of July 11, 1870; and to A. A. Lipscomb of February 15, 1886. Early titles of the poem— "After Tumult Rest" and "Quiet After the Storm"—had been changed to "The Inevitable Calm" when it was printed in *Youth's Companion*, LI (November 21, 1878), 402.

6. *Literary World*, XI (January 17, 1880), 24. On May 2, 1880, Swinburne expressed his "cordial thanks for the eloquent enthusiasm of your poetic praise." See Cecil Lang, ed., "Swinburne and American Literature: With Six Hitherto Unpublished Letters," *American Literature*, XIX (January, 1948), 348-49.

7. "Black Cudjo," to my knowledge, is the only Negro dialect verse that Hayne ever published. It should be noted that Page's "Marse Chan" appeared in 1884 and that Harris' Uncle Remus tales were published in the Atlanta *Constitution* as early as 1878. Of course, Negro dialect verse had appeared in some of the great monthlies before 1877. Thomas Dunn English, Lanier, and Russell all had contributed such verse by that year. See, for example, my article on English in *American Literature*, XXXIII (March, 1961), 72-75. Still,

Hayne maintained as late as 1884 in a letter to P. B. Marston that Cudjo's "patois is dying out, having only (so far as I know) been hitherto presented by myself." He also carefully pointed out that this dialect was "entirely different" from that of "the middle and up-country negroes."

8. See Claud B. Green, "Charles Colcock Jones, Jr. and Paul Hamilton Hayne," in *Georgians in Profile: Historical Essays in Honor of Ellis Merton Coulter*, ed. Horace Montgomery (Athens, 1958), pp. 248-49.

9. This stanza was left out of the text in *Harper's Monthly*, but Hayne restored it to the poem in the Complete Edition.

10. Moreover, at least three of the memorial poems—"On the Death of President Garfield," "Hiram H. Benner," and "The Death of Hood"—are actually laureate statements and are considered as such. "W. Gilmore Simms" might also be examined as a laureate poem but is primarily a memorial and is discussed accordingly.

11. For first printings of the three poems, see "Longfellow Dead," *Baldwin's Monthly*, XXIV (May, 1882), 5; "To Bayard Taylor Beyond Us," New-York *Tribune*, January 7, 1879; and "The Pole of Death: To the Memory of Sydney [*sic*] Lanier," *Harper's Monthly*, LXV (June, 1882), 98.

12. For a much revised partial draft of this poem, see the blank pages in the front and back of Hayne's copy of E. Lynn Linton's *The World Well Lost* (Philadelphia: J. B. Lippincott, 1878) in the Hayne Library, DUL. Many volumes in this collection contain drafts of Hayne's poems in various stages of completion.

13. The Hayne-Hazard friendship began in 1879 when the Haynes during their Northern trip visited Peace Dale, the Hazard estate near Newport, Rhode Island. From time to time thereafter Hazard contrived to send gifts of money in such tactful ways as not to offend Hayne's sense of pride.

14. Though Hayne was told that Georgia was to provide the "odeist" for the occasion, many (including Stedman) thought he was contributing as laureate of the South.

15. Claude R. Flory interprets the poem as an expression of a favorable view of the New South in the *Georgia Historical Quarterly*, XLVI (December, 1962), 388-94.

16. "Consummatum Est" appeared first in *Lippincott's Magazine*, XXIII (May, 1879), 619-20; "The Shadow of Death" in the *Sunday School Times*, XVIII (January 1, 1876), 1; "The True Heaven," "Twilight Monologue," and "In Harbor" were printed in *Harper's Monthly*, April, 1879, November, 1878, and July, 1882, respectively. "The True Heaven," though it obviously belongs with these poems, does not appear under the same heading. I have not been able to

locate the first appearance of "A Little While I Fain Would Linger Yet."

17. To this list might be added "Macdonald's Raid," "W. Gilmore Simms," "The Battle of King's Mountain," "The Return of Peace," the "Yorktown Centennial Lyric," and the three birthday tributes to Whittier, Holmes, and Emerson, but for reasons already given I have discussed them elsewhere.

18. The Stephens sonnet (*American*, February 25, 1882), for example, celebrates the statesman, the "man of Roman thought" and exemplar of a "race gone by," whose life had been based on the "antique virtues of a worthier day."

19. Hayne had written Holmes on April 6: "The political lyric embodies the passionate protest of my unfortunate compatriots, touching the monstrous tyranny of the Grant administration, which until 4 days ago we feared might be perpetuated. . . . Oh! Sir, if you could only imagine a *tenth* part of the anguish, the suffering, the *unmitigated torture* to which Carolinians have been subjected under 'Carpet Bag' & negro rule, you would even now stand aghast."

20. On December 29, 1884, Mrs. Ella F. Pratt, one of Lothrop's editors, wrote Hayne that the firm still wished to "defer" sending copies to reviewers. As to royalties, Will Hayne went to Boston in the fall of 1887, well over a year after his father's death, and collected "nearly a hundred dollars," the first payment from the publishing house, the officials of which promised for the fourth or fifth time to bring out a new and cheaper edition in which all the errors of 1882 would be corrected. When this edition failed to appear, young Hayne and his mother, through the good offices of H. W. Mabie, opened negotiations with Charles Scribner in New York. Scribner was willing to publish at his own risk a selected edition which would put Hayne's best work from his entire career in an "authoritative and final form." This proposal met with the approval of Mabie and the Haynes, but the plan fell through when Lothrop would not release the copyright for less than 8 percent on the sale of any edition published in New York. (Lothrop later offered to sell his rights for $1200, but Scribner thought this too high.)

Thus the Lothrop relationship proved in the long run to be a costly one to Hayne, for it prevented the publication of a selection of his verse and for all practical purposes put a stop to contemporary efforts to collect his last poems, to say nothing of what it did to his reputation by concentrating critical attention on an edition which, since none has succeeded it, has by default been taken as final and authoritative, yet which contains many printer's errors, has not been proofread by the author, is by any modern standard far too inclusive in its selection, and does not comprise the poet's latest work.

Chapter Six

1. Few of these poems have been discussed in the twentieth century. Excerpts from the "Sesqui-Centennial Ode" and the Charleston Centennial Poem are quoted in Charles W. Hubner, *Representative Southern Poets* (1906); Claud B. Green quotes from the "Ode" in "Charles Colcock Jones, Jr. and Paul Hamilton Hayne"; John A. Carter treats "To the New South" briefly in the *Georgia Historical Quarterly,* XLVIII (June, 1964), 193-95; and poems published in certain magazines after 1882 are considered in R. M. Atchison's "Southern Literary Magazines" and in my "Southern Writers and Northern Literary Magazines." The manuscript of "Last Poems" is in HP, DUL.

2. "Fallen!—Risen! On the Death of Senator B. H. Hill, of Georgia," *Home and Farm,* VII (September 15, 1882) [appeared first in the *Constitution*]; "Alexander Hamilton Stephens. In Memoriam," *Home and Farm,* VIII (April 1, 1883); "Charles Reade. In Memoriam," *The Independent,* XXXVI (July 17, 1884); "Victor Hugo," *The Independent,* XXXVII (June 11, 1885); "Gordon," *The Independent,* XXXVII (March 12, 1885); and " 'Habet,' " *The American,* X (June 27, 1885).

3. At this time the *Southern Bivouac* was bought by the owners of *Home and Farm,* and Hayne was invited to contribute by Knott, an editor of both periodicals. For an account of the *Bivouac,* see my article in *Southern Literary Journal* (Spring, 1970).

4. Some of Hayne's verse in *Home and Farm* is not collected in "Last Poems." See especially "The Farmer's Wife," February 1, 1882; "The Mocking Bird's Advent," April 1, 1882; "The First Farmer," January 15, 1883; "In Memoriam: Of Gen. James Conner, of South Carolina," July 15, 1883; "Lyric: Requested by the 'Southern Exposition,' at Louisville," October 1, 1883 [dedicated to R. W. Knott]; and "The Last Patch (of Cotton). A Landscape Study with a Moral," November 1, 1883. The last piece, another of Hayne's late poems dealing with the cash crop of the South, includes briefly a vignette (unusual for Hayne) of "Laborers" in the field:

> Yet, at the far field's southward end,
>> Next a broad reach of upland meadows,
> What forms are those that strangely blend,
>> Half lost amid the deepening shadows?
>
> A few old Laborers, toiling still—
>> And lo! pure white a flickering cluster,
> What lingering blooms, have graced the hill,
>> And crowned it with a star-soft lustre!

But a Longfellow-like moral at the end detracts from the lyric's better qualities. An incomplete version of this poem appeared recently in Rouse and Watkins, "Some Manuscript Poems of Paul Hamilton Hayne."

5. Printed by Atcheson L. Hench in *American Literature*, IV (May, 1932), 199-207. Blackmore also thought well of Hayne's poetry, as he had indicated earlier in letters of December 31, 1883, and August 16, 1884 (typed copies, HP, DUL).

Chapter Seven

1. Some of the conclusions of this chapter have also been propounded in my "Hayne the Poet: A New Look," *South Carolina Review* (November, 1969).

2. Edwin H. Cady, ed., *The American Poets: 1800-1900* (1966). Hayne's poetry has appeared recently in Jay B. Hubbell, ed., *American Life in Literature*, rev. ed., 2 vols. (1949); Lyon N. Richardson and others, eds., *The Heritage of American Literature*, 2 vols. (1951); Richmond C. Beatty and others, eds., *The Literature of the South* (1952); Leon Howard and others, eds., *American Heritage*, 2 vols. (1955); and Walter Blair and others, eds., *The Literature of the United States*, third ed., 2 vols. (1966). This list is, of course, not exhaustive; but it is representative of anthologies prepared for college audiences.

Selected Bibliography

PRIMARY SOURCES

1. Manuscripts—The Perkins Library of Duke University has the largest collection of Hayne manuscripts as well as the remains of the poet's library. Other holdings of importance are those at the Library of Congress, the New York Public Library, the Boston Public Library, and at libraries of the University of South Carolina, the University of North Carolina, the University of Virginia, the University of Texas, Cornell University, Columbia University, Yale University, Harvard University, and the Johns Hopkins University.

2. Books *(Volumes of poems are listed here in chronological order. Other works are cited in the text and notes.)*

Poems. Boston: Ticknor and Fields, 1855. Copyright 1854.

Sonnets, and Other Poems. Charleston: Harper & Calvo, 1857.

Avolio; A Legend of the Island of Cos. With Poems, Lyrical, Miscellaneous, and Dramatic. Boston: Ticknor and Fields, 1860. Copyright 1859.

Legends and Lyrics. Philadelphia: J. B. Lippincott & Co., 1872. Copyright 1871.

The Mountain of the Lovers; With Poems of Nature and Tradition. New York: E. J. Hale & Son, 1875.

Poems. Complete Edition. Boston: D. Lothrop and Co., 1882.

"Last Poems." Unpublished manuscript compiled and edited after Hayne's death by his wife and son (Duke University Library).

3. Letters. *(Major collections and two important lesser ones are listed.)*

A Collection of Hayne Letters, ed. Daniel M. McKeithan. Austin: University of Texas Press, 1944. Indispensable.

The Correspondence of Bayard Taylor and Paul Hamilton Hayne, ed. Charles Duffy. Baton Rouge: Louisiana State University Press, 1945.

"A Southern Genteelist: Letters of Paul Hamilton Hayne to Julia C. R. Dorr," ed. Charles Duffy, *South Carolina Historical and Genealogical Magazine,* LII (April, 1951), 65-73, to LIII (January, 1952), 19-30.

"Seven Unpublished Letters of Paul Hamilton Hayne," ed. William
S. Hoole, *Georgia Historical Quarterly*, XXII (September, 1938),
273-85. To Susan B. Hayne.
"Paul Hamilton Hayne to Dr. Francis Peyre Porcher," ed. Richard
B. Davis, *Studies in Philology*, XLIV (July, 1947), 529-48.

SECONDARY SOURCES

Strict space limitations preclude a full listing. Only items of particular value to this study are given; other materials are cited in the
text and notes. For Hayne bibliography, see Robert E. Spiller and
others, eds., *Literary History of the United States*, II (3rd ed., rev.,
(1963); and Louis D. Rubin, Jr., ed., *A Bibliographical Guide to the
Study of Southern Literature* (1969). See also Hubbell below.

ANDERSON, CHARLES. "Charles Gayarré and Paul Hayne: The Last
    Literary Cavaliers,"·*American Studies in Honor of William Ken-
    neth Boyd*, ed. David K. Jackson. Durham: Duke University
    Press, 1940.
GRIFFIN, MAX L. "Whittier and Hayne: A Record of Friendship,"
    American Literature, XIX (March, 1947) 41-58. Correspondence.
HUBBELL, JAY B., ed. *The Last Years of Henry Timrod*. Durham:
    Duke University Press, 1941. Very helpful on relations between
    Hayne and Timrod.
———. *The South in American Literature, 1607-1900*. Durham: Duke
    University Press, 1954. Standard literary history. Contains not
    only the best account of Hayne as man of letters but also the
    best bibliography of scholarship on Hayne to 1954.
LANIER, SIDNEY. *Works*. eds., Charles R. Anderson and others. Cen-
    tennial Edition. Baltimore: Johns Hopkins Press, 1945. 10 vols.
LEWISOHN, LUDWIG. "Paul Hamilton Hayne," "The Books We have
    Made," *The Sunday News* (Charleston, S.C.), September 20,
    1903, p. 20. Invaluable critical assessment of Hayne's poetry.
MCKEITHAN, DANIEL M., ed. *Selected Letters: John Garland James
    to Paul Hamilton Hayne and Mary Middleton Michel Hayne*.
    Austin: University of Texas Press, 1946.
———. "Paul Hamilton Hayne and *The Southern Bivouac*," University
    of Texas *Studies in English*, XVII (1937), 112-23.
———. "A Correspondence Journal of Paul Hamilton Hayne," *Georgia
    Historical Quarterly*, XXVI (September-December, 1942), 249-
    72. Very helpful on 1880-82.
MOORE, RAYBURN S. "Paul Hamilton Hayne," *Georgia Review*, XXII
    (Spring, 1968), 106-24. Sketches life and literary career.
———. "Hayne the Poet: A New Look." *South Carolina Review*, II
    (November, 1969), 4-13. Critical assessment.

PARKS, EDD W., ed. *Southern Poets.* New York: American Book Co., 1936. Excellent discussion of Hayne's poetry.

————. "When Paul Hamilton Hayne Fought a Duel," *Georgia Review,* XI (Spring, 1957), 1-5.

————. *Ante-Bellum Southern Literary Critics.* Athens: University of Georgia Press, 1962. Does not cover Hayne's later views, but still conveys range and scope of his opinions.

————. *Henry Timrod.* New York: Twayne Publishers, Inc., 1964, TUSAS. Contains much useful information on Hayne.

SIMMS, WILLIAM GILMORE, *The Letters,* eds., Mary C. Simms Oliphant and others. Columbia: University of South Carolina Press, 1952-56. 5 vols. For Hayne, see especially vols. III-V.

Index